LITTLE ★ HAPPY CIRCUS

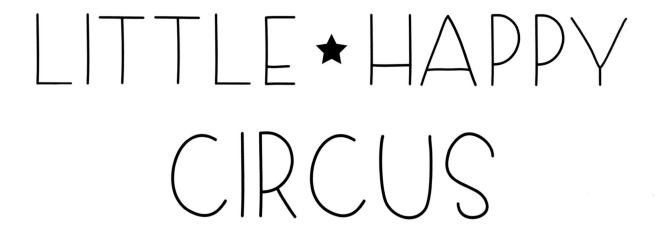

LITTLE ★ HAPPY CIRCUS

12 Amigurumi Crochet Toy Patterns for your
Favourite Circus Performers

TINE NIELSEN

www.sewandso.co.uk

CONTENTS

INTRODUCTION..6

WHAT YOU WILL NEED 8

BEFORE YOU GET STARTED 10

ABBREVIATIONS 12

CROCHET SCHOOL 14

ASSEMBLING 22

PATTERNS 26

• LITTLE MR. BEAR...............................28

• MR. HAPPY CIRCUS 34

• THE ADORABLE BALLERINA.............42

• SHINY MISS HORSE 48

• MR. ELEPHANT SLEEPYHEAD.............56

• LITTLE MISS MAGIC 62

• LITTLE YELLOW LION.........................70

• CLOWN OF THE DAY 76

• MR. STRONG.....................................84

• WALTER THE WALRUS 90

• GARLAND 98

• POPCORN..102

THANK YOU 106

SPONSORS AND SUPPLIERS 108

INDEX 110

INTRODUCTION

Come join us, the circus is in town! It's not just any circus, but the "Little Happy Circus".

Mr Happy Circus welcomes everyone happily. This circus is his whole life, and he is honoured to be able to entertain every single guest.

The Clown of the Day is a great help when it comes to entertaining the audience. Besides his blue nose, he has a very special talent for captivating and entertaining the audience.

The Adorable Ballerina dances elegantly right below the canvas ceiling of the circus tent. She really knows how to impress the audience with her pirouettes high up in the sky.

Shiny Miss Horse, the royal member of the circus family, can be seen under the spotlights. She is in no way a snooty character, although her movements are graceful and she loves impressing her audience.

If you're into loveliness, cuddling and friendships, you'll be very happy to meet Little Mr Bear and the Little Yellow Lion. They always spread joy and happiness around them.

Opposites attract as you'll see in the Little Happy Circus. Mr Elephant Sleepyhead, the biggest member of the circus, is best friends with Little Miss Magic, the smallest member of the circus. Little Miss Magic is also the most apprehensive member of the circus family. This is where Mr Elephant Sleepyhead comes to the rescue. He carries Miss Magic on his trunk, gently rocking her from side to side, to calm her nerves before every show.

Walter the Walrus loves circus tricks and playing with water. He is lucky enough to get a big kiss from one of the audience during some shows, but he secretly wishes it happened at every show.

Mr Strong is not just a strong man but also the crown prince of the Little Happy Circus. He is Mr Happy Circus's son and that's why the Little Happy Circus has a very special place in his heart.

If you wonder why this little circus is something quite unique, come and see it with your very own eyes. I promise you won't regret it!

WHAT YOU
WILL NEED

- · Yarn
- · Crochet hook
- · Stuffing
- · Safety eyes
- · Pair of scissors
- · Yarn needles
- · Pins
- · Feathers
- · Black sewing thread

YARN

I've chosen to use Drops yarn for all of the characters in the book, mainly Drops Safran and Drops Loves You 6. Yarnliving.com has been so kind to supply all of the yarn I've used to make this book.

You can use any yarn and any color to make the characters in this book. The choice of yarn is completely up to you and your preference.

I recommend that you use cotton yarn if the dolls are for children.

You can also differ the size of the dolls by using a thicker or thinner yarn. Just remember to use a crochet hook that fits the yarn. If you choose a different kind of yarn, be aware that the measurements of the dolls may change.

CROCHET HOOKS

There are so many crochet hooks available – I recommend that you use whichever one suits you. I prefer to use Clover Soft Touch crochet hooks and highly recommend them.

BEFORE YOU GET STARTED

STITCH MARKER

Use a stitch marker or a long strand of yarn in a contrasting color to mark the beginning of every round.

THE PATTERNS

On the next page you will find a list of the abbreviations used in the book.

You will also find a crochet school on page 14.
I've chosen not to show you the common stitches, such as chain, single crochet, etc. There are plenty of instructions and video tutorials available on the internet and Youtube.

All of the patterns in the book start with a description of the materials and abbreviations used in the particular pattern.

You are more than welcome to send me an email if you have any questions or if you need help following a pattern.

If there should be an error in any of the patterns, please let me know. You will find the corrections on my website at www.littlehappycrochet.dk

ABBREVIATIONS

· Chain stitch (ch)
· Slip stitch (sl st)
· Single crochet (sc)
· Half double crochet (hdc)
· Double crochet (dc)
· Double treble crochet (dtr)
· Increase (2i1)
· Decrease (2»1)
· Round (R)
· Row (RW)

CROCHET SCHOOL

Learn the ropes or improve your skills!

In addition to the basics of crochet, the simple techniques in our Crochet School will help you to create all of the patterns in this book.

POMPOM

Wrap the yarn around the fork until it's nice and thick. The more yarn you wrap, the thicker the pompom.

Cut a piece of yarn and insert the yarn between the middle tines of the fork. Remove the yarn from the fork.

Make a tight knot around the middle of the bundle. Cut all of the ends of the loops.

Now shake and roll the pompom between your hands. Trim it to make it nice and round.

CHANGING COLOR

Color changes are always difficult when crocheting in spiral. In my experience, color changes will never be completely invisible.

This is how I change color in spiral - it's often possible to hide the color changes under an arm or on the back of the doll when sewing parts together.

In the last stitch before the color change, you must use both the old and the new color.

Insert your crochet hook in the last stitch before the color change. You'll now have 2 loops on your hook.

Yarn over with the new color.

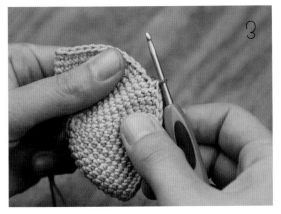

Pull the new yarn through the 2 loops. You're now set to continue with the new color.

This is how I do a color change.

DOUBLE TREBLE CROCHET

The double treble crochet is used for the lion's mane, amongst others.

Yarn over 3 times.

Insert your crochet hook into the stitch indicated, yarn over and pull a loop through. You'll now have 5 loops on your hook.

Yarn over and pull through the first 2 loops. You'll now have 4 loops on your hook.

Yarn over and pull through the next 2 loops. You'll now have 3 loops on your hook.

Yarn over and pull through the next 2 loops.
You'll now have 2 loops on your hook.

Yarn over and pull through the last 2 loops.
You've now made a double treble crochet.

For the lion's mane, you shift between double treble crochet and single crochet. Make a single crochet in the next stitch. Make sure that the "bump" is on the front of your work.

This is how it should look when you are alternating between double treble crochet and single crochet.

JOINING LEGS

For most of the dolls in this book, you need to join the legs together. It might seem a bit difficult at first if you haven't done this before, so I've included a photo tutorial to make it easier for you.

The photos below are of the circus director, however I use this technique to join the legs for all my dolls.

Don't break the yarn on the second leg. Chain 9.

Insert your crochet hook into any stitch on the first leg.

Crochet around the leg with 1 sc in each stitch.
For the circus director you will end up with 18 sc in total.

You've now reached the chain stitches.
Crochet 1 sc in each of the chain stitches = 9 sts

Crochet around the other leg with 1 sc in each stitch = 18 sts.

You've now reached the other side of the chain stitches. Crochet 1 sc in each of the chain stitches = 9 sts.

This is what the legs should look like now. For the circus director you should have 54 stitches in total.

ASSEMBLING

If you need to stuff the body parts as you go, the pattern will say so.

Please make sure you don't overstuff your doll as the stuffing will be visible through your work. Make sure to stuff the body parts evenly.

You can use pins to attach the body parts to make sure they're placed exactly as you wish. When you're happy with the look, sew the parts together.

Every pattern has a guide for assembling to help you end up with a nice result.

Please be aware to attach the parts thoroughly. You don't want the dolls to lose an arm or a leg during play. Personality comes from fine details - be patient and don't be afraid to have two or three tries before the result is satisfying to you.

PATTERNS

Welcome to the Little Happy Circus.

Enjoy magic moments in the company of clowns, acrobats and strong men along with our well-trained happy animals.

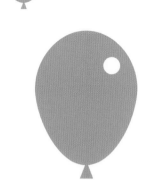

LITTLE MR. BEAR

WHAT YOU WILL NEED

MATERIALS

80 g of brown cotton
· Drops Safran, color 23

10 g of petrol blue cotton
· Drops Safran, color 51

A small amount of beige cotton
· Drops Safran, color 21

2 safety eyes, size 6 mm
Stuffing

2.5-3 mm

ABBREVIATIONS

Chain stitch (ch)
Slip stitch (sl st)
Single crochet (sc)
Increase (2i1)
Decrease (2»1)
Round (R)

Little Mr. Bear will measure
approx. 30 cm in height.

MR. BEAR IS THE NICEST
BEAR YOU WILL EVER
MEET. HE'S ALWAYS
UP FOR A CUDDLE.

LITTLE MR. BEAR

LEGS

· brown yarn (make 2)
Stuff as you go!
R1: 6 sc in a magic ring
= 6 sts
R2: (2i1) x 6 = 12 sts
R3: (3 sc, 2i1) x 3 = 15 sts
R4-7: sc around = 15 sts
R8: (4 sc, 2i1) x 3 = 18 sts
R9-12: sc around = 18 sts
R13: (2 sc, 2i1) x 6 = 24 sts
R14-15: sc around = 24 sts
Finish with a slip stitch. Break
the yarn and crochet the other
leg. Don't break the yarn on
the 2nd leg but continue
crocheting the body.

BODY

· brown yarn
Chain 5 and insert your hook in any
stitch on the first leg.
Crochet around that leg and continue
by crocheting around both the chain
stitches and the legs. You can find a
description on how to join legs on
page 20.

R16: 24 sc, 1 sc in each of the 5 chain
stitches, 24 sc, 1 sc in each of the 5
chain stitches = (58 sts)
R17: (28 sc, 2i1) x 2 = 60 sts
R18: (9 sc, 2i1) x 6 = 66 sts
R19: (10 sc, 2i1) x 6 = 72 sts
R20: (11 sc, 2i1) x 6 = 78 sts
R21: (12 sc, 2i1) x 6 = 84 sts
R22-31: sc around = 84 sts
R32: (12 sc, 2»1) x 6 = 78 sts
R33-34: sc around = 78 sts
R35: (11 sc, 2»1) x 6 = 72 sts
R36-37: sc around = 72 sts
R38: (10 sc, 2»1) x 6 = 66 sts
R39-40: sc around = 66 sts
R41: (9 sc, 2»1) x 6 = 60 sts
R42-43: sc around = 60 sts
R44: (8 sc, 2»1) x 6 = 54 sts
R45-47: sc around = 54 sts
R48: (7 sc, 2»1) x 6 = 48 sts
R49-51: sc around = 48 sts
R52: (6 sc, 2»1) x 6 = 42 sts
R53-55: sc around = 42 sts
R56: (5 sc, 2»1) x 6 = 36 sts
R57-59: sc around = 36 sts
R60: (4 sc, 2»1) x 6 = 30 sts
R61-63: sc around = 30 sts
R64: (3 sc, 2»1) x 6 = 24 sts
R65: sc around = 24 sts

R66: in the back loop only, sc around
= 24 sts
Finish with a slip stitch. Break the
yarn but leave enough yarn to sew
the head and the body together.

COLLAR

· petrol blue yarn
In round 66 you crocheted only in the
back loops. Now you will
have to start the collar in the
front loop on round 66.
Hold the bear so the legs are
pointing away from you. Make a
loop and insert your hook in any
stitch on the round.
R1: sc around = 24 sts
R2: (2i1) x 24 = 48 sts
R3: (2i1) x 48 = 96 sts
R4-9: sc around = 96 sts
Finish with a slip stitch. Break the
yarn and fasten off.

HEAD

· brown yarn
R1: 6 sc in a magic ring = 6 sts
R2: (2i1) x 6 = 12 sts
R3: (1 sc, 2i1) x 6 = 18 sts
R4: (2 sc, 2i1) x 6 = 24 sts
R5: (3 sc, 2i1) x 6 = 30 sts
R6: (4 sc, 2i1) x 6 = 36 sts
R7: (5 sc, 2i1) x 6 = 42 sts
R8: (6 sc, 2i1) x 6 = 48 sts
R9: (7 sc, 2i1) x 6 = 54 sts
R10: (8 sc, 2i1) x 6 = 60 sts
R11: (9 sc, 2i1) x 6 = 66 sts
R12: (10 sc, 2i1) x 6 = 72 sts
R13-24: sc around = 72 sts
Insert your safety eyes at this point. They should be placed between rounds 13 and 14 and with 7 sc between them.
R25: (10 sc, 2»1) x 6 = 66 sts
R26: (9 sc, 2»1) x 6 = 60 sts
R27: (8 sc, 2»1) x 6 = 54 sts
R28: (7 sc, 2»1) x 6 = 48 sts
R29: (6 sc, 2»1) x 6 = 42 sts
R30: (5 sc, 2»1) x 6 = 36 sts
R31: (4 sc, 2»1) x 6 = 30 sts
R32: (3 sc, 2»1) x 6 = 24 sts
Finish with a slip stitch and break the yarn.

MUZZLE

· beige yarn
R1: 6 sc in a magic ring = 6 sts
R2: (2i1) x 6 = 12 sts
R3: (1 sc, 2i1) x 6 = 18 sts
R4: (2 sc, 2i1) x 6 = 24 sts
R5: (3 sc, 2i1) x 6 = 30 sts
R6: (4 sc, 2i1) x 6 = 36 sts
Finish with a slip stitch. Break the yarn but leave enough to sew the muzzle onto the head.

ARMS

· brown yarn (make 2)
R1: 6 sc in a magic ring = 6 sts
R2: (2i1) x 6 = 12 sts
R3: (2 sc, 2i1) x 4 = 16 sts
R4-24: sc around = 16 sts
R25: (6 sc, 2»1) x 2 = 14 sts
R26: sc around = 14 sts
Finish with a slip stitch. Break the yarn but leave enough to sew the arm onto the body.

TAIL

· brown yarn
R1: 6 sc in a magic ring = 6 sts
R2: (2i1) x 6 = 12 sts
R3-5: sc around = 12 sts
R6: (2»1) x 6 = 6 sts
Finish with a slip stitch. Break the yarn but leave enough to sew the tail onto the body.

EARS

· brown yarn (make 2)
R1: 6 sc in a magic ring = 6 sts
R2: (2i1) x 6 = 12 sts
R3: (1 sc, 2i1) x 6 = 18 sts
R4: (2 sc, 2i1) x 6 = 24 sts
R5-8: sc around = 24 sts
R9: (2 sc, 2»1) x 6 = 18 sts
R10: sc around = 18 sts
Finish with a slip stitch. Break the yarn but leave enough to sew the ear onto the head.

ASSEMBLING

1.
Stuff the head and embroider the nose and the mouth on the muzzle.
See picture A.
Pin the muzzle to the head and sew it on.

2.
Bend the ears a bit and sew them onto the top of the head. They should be placed between rounds 7 and 15. See picture B.

3.
Sew the head and the body together. Make sure to stuff the neck before sewing all the way around. It'll keep the head from dangling.

4.
Stuff the arms but not all the way to the top. Sew them onto each side of the body, 3 rounds from the collar.
See picture C.

5.
Stuff the tail and sew it onto the back of the body. Place it between round 29 and round 31. See picture D.

LITTLE
MR. BEAR

MR. HAPPY CIRCUS

WHAT YOU WILL NEED

MATERIALS
18 g of jeans blue cotton
· Drops Safran, color 06

35 g of black cotton
· Drops Safran, color 16

20 g of off white cotton
· Drops Safran, color 18

A small amount of curry yellow cotton
· Drops Loves You 6, color 105

2 safety eyes, size 6 mm
Stuffing
Cardboard/plastic to stabilize the hat
8 safety eyes for the rows of buttons (optional)

2.5-3 mm

ABBREVIATIONS
Chain stitch (ch)
Slip stitch (sl st)
Single crochet (sc)
Half double crochet (hdc)
Double crochet (dc)
Increase (2i1)
Decrease (2»1)
Round (R)
Row (RW)

Mr. Happy Circus will measure
approx. 30 cm in height.

WITH HIS HAT SLIGHTLY
TILTED AND HIS
MOUSTACHE PERFECTLY
TRIMMED, MR. HAPPY
CIRCUS WELCOMES
EVERYONE TO THE
HAPPIEST CIRCUS
OF THEM ALL.

MR. HAPPY CIRCUS

Double row of buttons: I've chosen to use safety eyes as buttons with embroidery in between. You can also embroider french knots as buttons.
If you choose to use safety eyes, you'll have to insert them as you go. The first two safety eyes should be placed between rounds 36 and 37 and with 6 sc between them. Place each remaining set of 2 buttons 5 rounds above the last.

LEGS
· jeans blue yarn (make 2)
Stuff as you go!
R1: 6 sc in a magic ring = 6 sts
R2: (2i1) x 6 = 12 sts
R3: (1 sc, 2i1) x 6 = 18 sts
R4-15: sc around = 18 sts
Finish with a slip stitch. Break the yarn and crochet the other leg. Don't break the yarn on the 2nd leg but continue crocheting the body.

BODY
· jeans blue yarn
Chain 9 and insert your hook in any stitch on the first leg.
Crochet around that leg and continue by crocheting around both the chain stitches and the legs. You can find a description on page 20 on how to join legs.
R16: 18 sc, 1 sc in each of the 9 chain stitches, 18 sc, 1 sc in each of the 9 chain stitches = 54 sts
R17: (8 sc, 2i1) x 6 = 60 sts
R18: sc around = 60 sts
R19: (9 sc, 2i1) x 6 = 66 sts
R20: sc around = 66 sts
R21: (10 sc, 2i1) x 6 = 72 sts
R22: sc around = 72 sts
R23: (11 sc, 2i1) x 6 = 78 sts
R24: sc around = 78 sts
R25: (12 sc, 2i1) x 6 = 84 sts
R26-28: sc around = 84 sts
Change to black yarn
R29: sc around = 84 sts
R30: in the back loop only, sc around = 84 sts
R31-38: sc around = 84 sts
R39: (12 sc, 2»1) x 6 = 78 sts
R40: sc around = 78 sts
R41: (11 sc, 2»1) x 6 = 72 sts
R42: sc around = 72 sts
R43: (10 sc, 2»1) x 6 = 66 sts
R44: sc around = 66 sts
R45: (9 sc, 2»1) x 6 = 60 sts
R46: sc around = 60 sts
R47: (8 sc, 2»1) x 6 = 54 sts
R48: sc around = 54 sts
R49: (7 sc, 2»1) x 6 = 48 sts
R50: sc around = 48 sts
R51: (6 sc, 2»1) x 6 = 42 sts
R52: sc around = 42 sts
R53: (5 sc, 2»1) x 6 = 36 sts
R54-55: sc around = 36 sts
R56: (4 sc, 2»1) x 6 = 30 sts
R57: sc around = 30 sts
R58: sc around = 30 sts
Finish with a slip stitch. Break the yarn but leave enough to sew the body and head together.

EDGE, JACKET
· black yarn
In round 30 on the body you crocheted only in the back loops.
Now you'll have to crochet in the front loops. Turn the legs away from you.
Insert your hook in any stitch and sc around = 84 sts

HEAD
· off-white yarn
R1: 6 sc in a magic ring = 6 sts
R2: (2i1) x 6 = 12 sts
R3: (1 sc, 2i1) x 6 = 18 sts
R4: (2 sc, 2i1) x 6 = 24 sts
R5: (3 sc, 2i1) x 6 = 30 sts
R6: (4 sc, 2i1) x 6 = 36 sts
R7: (5 sc, 2i1) x 6 = 42 sts

R8: (6 sc, 2i1) x 6 = 48 sts
R9: (7 sc, 2i1) x 6 = 54 sts
R10: (8 sc, 2i1) x 6 = 60 sts
R11: (9 sc, 2i1) x 6 = 66 sts
R12: (10 sc, 2i1) x 6 = 72 sts
R13-23: sc around = 72 sts
Insert your safety eyes at this point. They should be placed between rounds 15 and 16 and with 5 sc between them.
R24: (10 sc, 2»1) x 6 = 66 sts
R25: sc around = 66 sts
R26: (9 sc, 2»1) x 6 = 60 sts
R27: sc around = 60 sts
R28: (8 sc, 2»1) x 6 = 54 sts
R29: (7 sc, 2»1) x 6 = 48 sts
R30: (6 sc, 2»1) x 6 = 42 sts
R31: (5 sc, 2»1) x 6 = 36 sts
R32: (4 sc, 2»1) x 6 = 30 sts
Finish with a slip stitch and break the yarn.

ARMS

· off-white yarn (make 2)
Stuff as you go!
R1: 6 sc in a magic ring = 6 sts
R2: (2i1) x 6 = 12 sts
R3-5: sc around = 12 sts
Change to black yarn
R6: sc around = 12 sts
R7: in the back loop only,
sc around = 12 sts
R8-37: sc around = 12 sts
Finish with a slip stitch. Break the yarn but leave enough to sew the arm onto the body.

EDGE, SLEEVE

· black yarn (make 2)
In round 7 on the arm you crocheted only in the back loops. Now you'll have to crochet in the front loop. Turn the hand away from you.
Insert your hook in any stitch and sc around = 12 sts

MOUSTACHE

· black yarn
Chain 17. Start at the 2nd chain stitch from the hook.
Rw1: 2 sl st, 1 sc, 1 hdc, 2 dc, 1 hdc, 1 sc, 1 sl st, 1 hdc, 2 dc, 1 hdc, 1 sc, 2 sl st = 16 sts
Break the yarn but leave enough to sew the moustache to the head.

HAT

· black yarn
R1: 6 sc in a magic ring = 6 sts
R2: (2i1) x 6 = 12 sts
R3: (1 sc, 2i1) x 6 = 18 sts
R4: (2 sc, 2i1) x 6 = 24 sts
R5: (3 sc, 2i1) x 6 = 30 sts
Before continuing, draw the circle onto a piece of cardboard/plastic. You'll need it to stabilize the bottom of the hat.

R6: in the back loop only,
sc around = 30 sts
R7-8: sc around = 30 sts
R9: (3 sc, 2»1) x 6 = 24 sts
R10-11: sc around = 24 sts
R12: (3 sc, 2i1) x 6 = 30 sts
R13-14: sc around = 30 sts
R15: in the front loop only,
sc around = 30 sts
R16: (4 sc, 2i1) x 6 = 36 sts
R17: (5 sc, 2i1) x 6 = 42 sts
Finish with a slip stitch. Break the yarn but leave enough to sew the hat onto the head.

WHIP

· black yarn
The whip is crocheted in rows and each row is turned with 1 chain stitch.
Chain 16. Start in the 2nd chain stitch from the hook.
Rw1-3: sc to end = 15 sts
Finish with a slip stitch. Break the yarn but leave about 40 cm. Fold the whip and sew it together along the edge. Fasten off and use the end of the yarn as the whip itself.

ASSEMBLING

1.

Stuff the head. Pin the moustache to the head and sew it on.
The moustache should be placed one round below the eyes. See picture A.

2.

Sew the head and the body together, Make sure to stuff the neck properly before sewing all the way around. It keeps the head from dangling.

3.

Sew the arms onto each side of the body at the neck. See picture B.

4.

Place the cardboard/plastic in the bottom of the hat and stuff it. Pin the hat to the head slightly tilted and sew it on.
See picture C.

5.

Embroider cross stitches between the safety eyes with curry yellow yarn. See picture D.
If you do not want to use safety eyes as buttons, you can embroider french knots instead.

THE ADORABLE BALLERINA

WHAT YOU WILL NEED

MATERIALS
45 g of off-white cotton
· Drops Safran, color 18

75 g of light pink cotton
· Drops Safran, color 01

15 g of brown cotton
· Drops Safran, color 23

A small amount of black cotton
· Drops Safran, color 16

2 safety eyes, size 6 mm
Stuffing

2.5-3 mm

ABBREVIATIONS
Chain stitch (ch)
Slip stitch (sl st)
Single crochet (sc)
Half double crochet (hdc)
Double crochet (dc)
Increase (2i1)
Decrease (2»1)
Round (R)

The Adorable Ballerina will measure approx.
40 cm in height and 25 cm when sitting.

WHEN THE ADORABLE
BALLERINA IS BALANCING
ON THE WIRE, JUST BELOW
THE CEILING OF THE CIRCUS
TENT, SHE IS SO HAPPY.
SHE CAN'T IMAGINE LIFE
WITHOUT THE LITTLE
HAPPY CIRCUS.

THE ADORABLE BALLERINA

HEAD
· off-white
Stuff as you go!
R1: 6 sc in a magic ring = 6 sts
R2: (2i1) x 6 = 12 sts
R3: (1 sc, 2i1) x 6 = 18 sts
R4: (2 sc, 2i1) x 6 = 24 sts
R5: (3 sc, 2i1) x 6 = 30 sts
R6: (4 sc, 2i1) x 6 = 36 sts
R7: (5 sc, 2i1) x 6 = 42 sts
R8: (6 sc, 2i1) x 6 = 48 sts
R9: (7 sc, 2i1) x 6 = 54 sts
R10: (8 sc, 2i1) x 6 = 60 sts
R11: (9 sc, 2i1) x 6 = 66 sts
R12-22: sc around = 66 sts
Insert your safety eyes at this point. They should be placed between rounds 13 and 14 and with 6 sc between them.
R23: (9 sc, 2»1) x 6 = 60 sts
R24: (8 sc, 2»1) x 6 = 54 sts
R25: (7 sc, 2»1) x 6 = 48 sts
R26: (6 sc, 2»1) x 6 = 42 sts
R27: (5 sc, 2»1) x 6 = 36 sts
R28: (4 sc, 2»1) x 6 = 30 sts
R29: (3 sc, 2»1) x 6 = 24 sts
R30: sc around = 24 sts
Finish with a slip stitch and break the yarn.

BODY
· light pink yarn
Stuff as you go!
R1: 6 sc in a magic ring = 6 sts
R2: (2i1) x 6 = 12 sts
R3: (1 sc, 2i1) x 6 = 18 sts
R4: (2 sc, 2i1) x 6 = 24 sts
R5: (3 sc, 2i1) x 6 = 30 sts
R6: (4 sc, 2i1) x 6 = 36 sts
R7: (5 sc, 2i1) x 6 = 42 sts
R8: (6 sc, 2i1) x 6 = 48 sts
R9: (7 sc, 2i1) x 6 = 54 sts
R10: (8 sc, 2i1) x 6 = 60 sts
R11: (9 sc, 2i1) x 6 = 66 sts
R12: (10 sc, 2i1) x 6 = 72 sts
R13-20: sc around = 72 sts
R21: (10 sc, 2»1) x 6 = 66 sts
R22-23: sc around = 66 sts
R24: in the back loop only, sc around = 66 sts
R25: sc around = 66 sts
R26: (9 sc, 2»1) x 6 = 60 sts
R27-30: sc around = 60 sts
R31: (8 sc, 2»1) x 6 = 54 sts
R32-35: sc around = 54 sts
R36: (7 sc, 2»1) x 6 = 48 sts
R37-40: sc around = 48 sts
R41: (6 sc, 2»1) x 6 = 42 sts
R42-44: sc around = 42 sts
Change to off-white yarn

R45: in the back loop only, sc around = 42 sts
R46: (5 sc, 2»1) x 6 = 36 sts
R47-49: sc around = 36 sts
R50: (4 sc, 2»1) x 6 = 30 sts
R51: (3 sc, 2»1) x 6 = 24 sts
Finish with a slip stitch. Break the yarn but leave enough to sew the body and the head together.

SKIRT
· light pink yarn
You crocheted in the back loop only in round 24 on the body. Now you will have to crochet in the front loop. Hold the bottom of the body away from you. Insert your hook in any stitch on the body and sc around = 66 sts
R1: sc around = 66 sts
R2: (2i1) x 66 = 132 sts
R3: sc around = 132 sts
R4: (1 sc, 2i1) x 66 = 198 sts
R5-10: sc around = 198 sts
Finish with a slip stitch. Break the yarn and fasten off.

HAIR

· brown yarn
R1: 6 sc in a magic ring = 6 sts
R2: (2i1) x 6 = 12 sts
R3: (1 sc, 2i1) x 6 = 18 sts
R4: (2 sc, 2i1) x 6 = 24 sts
R5: (3 sc, 2i1) x 6 = 30 sts
R6: (4 sc, 2i1) x 6 = 36 sts
R7: (5 sc, 2i1) x 6 = 42 sts
R8: (6 sc, 2i1) x 6 = 48 sts
R9: (7 sc, 2i1) x 6 = 54 sts
R10: (8 sc, 2i1) x 6 = 60 sts
R11: (9 sc, 2i1) x 6 = 66 sts
R12-20: sc around = 66 sts
R21: 57 sc, 1 hdc, 5 dc, 1
hdc, 1 sc, 1 sl st = 66 sts
Finish with a slip stitch. Break
the yarn but leave enough to
sew the hair onto the head.

BUN

· brown yarn
R1: 6 sc in a magic ring = 6 sts
R2: (2i1) x 6 = 12 sts
R3: (1 sc, 2i1) x 6 = 18 sts
R4: (2 sc, 2i1) x 6 = 24 sts
R5: (3 sc, 2i1) x 6 = 30 sts
R6: (4 sc, 2i1) x 6 = 36 sts
R7: (5 sc, 2i1) x 6 = 42 sts
R8: (6 sc, 2i1) x 6 = 48 sts
R9-13: sc around = 48 sts
R14: (6 sc, 2»1) x 6 = 42 sts
Finish with a slip stitch. Break the
yarn but leave enough to sew the
bun onto the hair.

ARMS

· off-white yarn (make 2)
Stuff as you go but make sure not to
stuff all the way to the top.
R1: 6 sc in a magic ring = 6 sts
R2: (2i1) x 6 = 12 sts
R3-46: sc around = 12 sts
Finish with a slip stitch. Break
the yarn but leave enough to
sew the arm to the body.

LEGS

· black yarn (make 2)
Stuff as you go!
R1: 6 sc in a magic ring = 6 sts
R2: (2i1) x 6 = 12 sts
R3-6: sc around = 12 sts
Change to off-white yarn
R7-46: sc around = 12 sts
Change to light pink yarn
R47-50: sc around = 12 sts
Finish with a slip stitch. Break
the yarn but leave enough to
sew the leg to the body.

ASSEMBLING

1.

Pin the hair to the head and place it so she will get a side parting. Sew the hair all the way around. Please be aware not to sew it too tight as the edge of the hair might get uneven. See picture A.

2.

Stuff the bun and pin it to the hair, 12 rounds from the edge. Sew it on all the way around.

3.

Embroider a little nose with off-white yarn by stitching 2-5 times over 2 stitches. Embroider the nose 3 rounds below the eyes. See picture B.

4.

Sew the head and the body together. Make sure to stuff the neck properly before sewing all the way around. It keeps the head from dangling.

5.

Sew the arms onto each side of the body, 2 rounds below the neck. Thread a needle with a long string of light pink yarn and sew the straps of the dress. See picture C.

6.

Pin the legs onto the bottom of the body and sew them on. Thread a needle with black yarn and embroider the straps on the legs. See picture D.

THE ADORABLE
BALLERINA

SHINY MISS HORSE

WHAT YOU WILL NEED

MATERIALS

120 g of coal grey cotton
· Drops Loves You 6, color 118

30 g of off-white cotton
· Drops Loves You 6, color 101

A small amount of light grey cotton
· Drops Loves You 6, color 103

2.5-3 mm

Some silver thread for the halter
2 safety eyes, size 12 mm
Feathers
Stuffing

ABBREVIATIONS

Chain stitch (ch)
Slip stitch (sl st)
Single crochet (sc)
Increase (2i1)
Decrease (2»1)
Round (R)
Row (RW)

Shiny Miss Horse will measure
approx. 35 cm in height.

SHINY MISS HORSE BRINGS
SHINE AND COLOR TO THE
CIRCUS. SHE LOVES FRINGES,
FEATHERS AND FIREWORKS.
EVERY DAY IS A GIFT AND
MUST BE CELEBRATED.

SHINY MISS HORSE

LEGS

· coal grey yarn (make 2)
Stuff as you go!
R1: 6 sc in a magic ring = 6 sts
R2: (2i1) x 6 = 12 sts
R3: (3 sc, 2i1) x 3 = 15 sts
R4-7: sc around = 15 sts
R8: (4 sc, 2i1) x 3 = 18 sts
R9-12: sc around = 18 sts
R13: (2 sc, 2i1) x 6 = 24 sts
R14-15: sc around = 24 sts
Finish with a slip stitch. Break the yarn and crochet the other leg. Don't break the yarn on the 2nd leg but continue crocheting the body.

BODY

· coal grey yarn
Chain 5 and insert your hook in any stitch on the first leg. Crochet around that leg and continue by crocheting around both the chain stitches and the legs. You can find a description on page 20 on how to join legs.
R16: 24 sc, 1 sc in each of the 5 chain stitches, 24 sc, 1 sc in each of the 5 chain stitches = 58 sts
R17: (28 sc, 2i1) x 2 = 60 sts
R18: (9 sc, 2i1) x 6 = 66 sts

R19: (10 sc, 2i1) x 6 = 72 sts
R20: (11 sc, 2i1) x 6 = 78 sts
R21: (12 sc, 2i1) x 6 = 84 sts
R22-31: sc around = 84 sts
R32: (12 sc, 2»1) x 6 = 78 sts
R33-34: sc around = 78 sts
R35: (11 sc, 2»1) x 6 = 72 sts
R36-37: sc around = 72 sts
R38: (10 sc, 2»1) x 6 = 66 sts
R39-40: sc around = 66 sts
R41: (9 sc, 2»1) x 6 = 60 sts
R42-43: sc around = 60 sts
R44: (8 sc, 2»1) x 6 = 54 sts
R45-47: sc around = 54 sts
R48: (7 sc, 2»1) x 6 = 48 sts
R49-51: sc around = 48 sts
R52: (6 sc, 2»1) x 6 = 42 sts
R53-55: sc around = 42 sts
R56: (5 sc, 2»1) x 6 = 36 sts
R57-59: sc around = 36 sts
R60: (4 sc, 2»1) x 6 = 30 sts
R61-63: sc around = 30 sts
R64: (3 sc, 2»1) x 6 = 24 sts
R65-66: sc around = 24 sts
Finish with a slip stitch.
Break the yarn but leave enough to sew the body and the head together.

HEAD

· off-white yarn
Stuff as you go!
R1: 6 sc in a magic ring = 6 sts
R2: (2i1) x 6 = 12 sts
R3: (1 sc, 2i1) x 6 = 18 sts
R4: (2 sc, 2i1) x 6 = 24 sts
R5: (3 sc, 2i1) x 6 = 30 sts
R6: (4 sc, 2i1) x 6 = 36 sts
R7: (5 sc, 2i1) x 6 = 42 sts
R8-10: sc around = 42 sts
Change to coal grey yarn
R11-12: sc around = 42 sts
R13: (6 sc, 2i1) x 6 = 48 sts
R14-16: sc around = 48 sts
R17: (7 sc, 2i1) x 6 = 54 sts
R18-20: sc around = 54 sts
R21: (8 sc, 2i1) x 6 = 60 sts
R22-24: sc around = 60 sts
R25: (9 sc, 2i1) x 6 = 66 sts
R26-35: sc around = 66 sts
Insert your safety eyes at this point. They should be placed between rounds 26 and 27 and with 15 sc between them.
R36: (9 sc, 2»1) x 6 = 60 sts
R37: sc around = 60 sts
R38: (8 sc, 2»1) x 6 = 54 sts
R39: (7 sc, 2»1) x 6 = 48 sts
R40: (6 sc, 2»1) x 6 = 42 sts
R41: (5 sc, 2»1) x 6 = 36 sts

R42: (4 sc, 2»1) x 6 = 30 sts
R43: (3 sc, 2»1) x 6 = 24 sts
R44: (2 sc, 2»1) x 6 = 18 sts
R45: (1 sc, 2»1) x 6 = 12 sts
R46: (2»1) x 6 = 6 sts
Finish with a slip stitch. Break the
yarn but leave enough to
sew the hole together. Sew the
hole by stitching in the front loop
of the 5 sc. Pull the thread so the
hole closes in. Fasten off.

EARS

· coal grey yarn (make 2)
R1: 6 sc in a magic ring = 6 sts
R2: sc around = 6 sts
R3: (2i1) x 6 = 12 sts
R4-5: sc around = 12 sts
R6: (1 sc, 2i1) x 6 = 18 sts
R7-10: sc around = 18 sts
Finish with a slip stitch. Break the
yarn but leave enough to sew the
ear onto the head.

ARMS

· coal grey yarn (make 2)
R1: 6 sc in a magic ring = 6 sts
R2: (2i1) x 6 = 12 sts
R3: (2 sc, 2i1) x 4 = 16 sts
R4-24: sc around = 16 sts
R25: (6 sc, 2»1) x 2 = 14 sts
R26: sc around = 14 sts
Finish with a slip stitch. Break the
yarn but leave enough to sew the
arm to the body.

HALTER

The halter is crocheted in both light
grey yarn and the silver thread.
The halter is crocheted in rows. Turn
each row with 1 chain stitch.

HALTER
MUZZLE PIECE

· light grey yarn and silver thread
Chain 45 with both the light grey
yarn and the silver thread.
Start in the 2nd chain stitch from
the hook.
Rw1: sc to end = 44 sts
Fasten off, leaving enough to sew
the halter onto the muzzle.

HALTER
NECK PIECE

· light grey yarn and silver thread
Chain 65 with both the light grey
yarn and the silver thread. Start in
the 2nd chain stitch from the hook.
Rw1: sc to end = 64 sts
Fasten off, leaving enough to sew
the halter onto the head.

HALTER
FOREHEAD PIECE

· light grey yarn and silver thread
Chain 29 with both the light grey
yarn and the silver thread.
Start in the 2nd chain stitch from
the hook.
Rw1: sc to end = 28 sts
Fasten off, leaving enough to sew
the halter onto the forehead.

FEATHER
HOLDER

· light grey yarn
R1: 6 sc in a magic ring = 6 sts
R2-7: sc around = 6 sts
Finish with a slip stitch. Break the
yarn but leave enough to sew the
holder onto the head.

ASSEMBLING

1.
Pin the head to the body to make sure it's placed correctly. Sew the head and body together. Stuff the neck before sewing all the way around to keep the head from dangling.

2.
Sew the ears onto the top of the head. Attach them at round 35 and with 11 stitches between them. See picture A.

3.
Stuff the arms but not all the way to the top. Sew them onto each side of the body, 5 rounds below the neck.

4.
It's now time to attach the halter. Place the strap around the muzzle right where the color changes. Sew the 2 ends together. I've also given it a few stitches below the muzzle, so the halter doesn't move.
Sew the strap for the neck onto each side of the halter and sew the strap for the forehead on, just below the ears.
Sew in all ends.
See picture B.

5.
Giving the horse a mane: cut a bunch of long strands of yarn, approx. 30 cm long. Use pins to mark where you want the mane to be placed. Start between the ears and continue until 6 rounds above the neck. Crochet one strand of hair at a time from between the ears to the neck. Continue with another 3 rows of hair on each side of the beginning row, or until you think there's enough hair. See picture C.
Trim the hair if you're going for a more groomed look.

6.
Cut a bunch of strands of yarn for the tail, approx. 50 cm long. Attach each strand of yarn at the back of the horse, at round 30 from the legs. Make a braid. See picture D.

7.
Sew the feather holder onto the head right between the ears. Place the feathers in the holder.

MR. ELEPHANT SLEEPYHEAD

WHAT YOU WILL NEED

MATERIALS
170 g of light grey cotton
· Drops Loves You 6, color 103

A small amount of coal grey cotton
· Drops Loves You 6, color 118

A small amount of sea green cotton
· Drops Loves You 6, color 112

A small amount of jeans blue cotton
· Drops Loves You 6, color 117

Stuffing

 2.5-3 mm

ABBREVIATIONS
Chain stitch (ch)
Slip stitch (sl st)
Single crochet (sc)
Increase (2i1)
Decrease (2»1)
Round (R)

Mr. Elephant Sleepyhead will measure approx. 30 cm in height.

I MEAN, IT'S NOT THAT MR. ELEPHANT SLEEPYHEAD FINDS THE CIRCUS LIFE BORING - ON THE CONTRARY. IT'S JUST THAT THERE'S ALWAYS A NAP THAT'S CALLING FOR HIM.

MR. ELEPHANT SLEEPYHEAD

LEGS

· light grey yarn (make 2)
Stuff as you go!
R1: 6 sc in a magic ring = 6 sts
R2: (2i1) x 6 = 12 sts
R3: (3 sc, 2i1) x 3 = 15 sts
R4-7: sc around = 15 sts
R8: (4 sc, 2i1) x 3 = 18 sts
R9-12: sc around = 18 sts
R13: (2 sc, 2i1) x 6 = 24 sts
R14-15: sc around = 24 sts
Finish with a slip stitch. Break the yarn and crochet the other leg. Don't break the yarn on the 2nd leg but continue crocheting the body.

BODY

· light grey yarn
Chain 5 and insert your hook in any stitch on the first leg.
Crochet around that leg and continue by crocheting around both the chain stitches and the legs. You can find a description on page 20 on how to join legs.
R16: 24 sc, 1 sc in each of the 5 chain stitches, 24 sc, 1 sc in each of the 5 chain stitches = 58 sts

R17: (28 sc, 2i1) x 2 = 60 sts
R18: (9 sc, 2i1) x 6 = 66 sts
R19: (10 sc, 2i1) x 6 = 72 sts
R20: (11 sc, 2i1) x 6 = 78 sts
R21: (12 sc, 2i1) x 6 = 84 sts
R22-31: sc around = 84 sts
R32: (12 sc, 2»1) x 6 = 78 sts
R33-34: sc around = 78 sts
R35: (11 sc, 2»1) x 6 = 72 sts
R36-37: sc around = 72 sts
R38: (10 sc, 2»1) x 6 = 66 sts
R39-40: sc around = 66 sts
R41: (9 sc, 2»1) x 6 = 60 sts
R42-43: sc around = 60 sts
R44: (8 sc, 2»1) x 6 = 54 sts
R45-47: sc around = 54 sts
R48: (7 sc, 2»1) x 6 = 48 sts
R49-51: sc around = 48 sts
R52: (6 sc, 2»1) x 6 = 42 sts
R53-55: sc around = 42 sts
R56: (5 sc, 2»1) x 6 = 36 sts
R57-59: sc around = 36 sts
R60: (4 sc, 2»1) x 6 = 30 sts
R61-63: sc around = 30 sts
R64: (3 sc, 2»1) x 6 = 24 sts
R65-66: sc around = 24 sts
Finish with a slip stitch. Break the yarn but leave enough to sew the body and the head together.

HEAD

· light grey yarn
Stuff as you go!
R1: 6 sc in a magic ring = 6 sts
R2: (2i1) x 6 = 12 sts
R3-20: sc around = 12 sts
R21: (5 sc, 2i1) x 2 = 14 sts
R22-23: sc around = 14 sts
R24: (6 sc, 2i1) x 2 = 16 sts
R25-26: sc around = 16 sts
R27: (7 sc, 2i1) x 2 = 18 sts
R28-29: sc around = 18 sts
R30: (2 sc, 2i1) x 6 = 24 sts
R31-32: sc around = 24 sts
R33: (3 sc, 2i1) x 6 = 30 sts
R34-35: sc around = 30 sts
R36: (4 sc, 2i1) x 6 = 36 sts
R37: sc around = 36 sts
R38: (5 sc, 2i1) x 6 = 42 sts
R39: (6 sc, 2i1) x 6 = 48 sts
R40: (7 sc, 2i1) x 6 = 54 sts
R41: (8 sc, 2i1) x 6 = 60 sts
R42: (9 sc, 2i1) x 6 = 66 sts
R43: (10 sc, 2i1) x 6 = 72 sts
R44-55: sc around = 72 sts
R56: (10 sc, 2»1) x 6 = 66 sts
R57: sc around = 66 sts
R58: (9 sc, 2»1) x 6 = 60 sts
R59: sc around = 60 sts

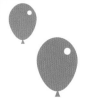

R60: (8 sc, 2»1) x 6 = 54 sts
R61: sc around = 54 sts
R62: (7 sc, 2»1) x 6 = 48 sts
R63: (6 sc, 2»1) x 6 = 42 sts
R64: (5 sc, 2»1) x 6 = 36 sts
R65: (4 sc, 2»1) x 6 = 30 sts
R66: (3 sc, 2»1) x 6 = 24 sts
R67: (2 sc, 2»1) x 6 = 18 sts
R68: (1 sc, 2»1) x 6 = 12 sts
R69: (2»1) x 6 = 6 sts
Finish with a slip stitch. Break the
yarn but leave enough to sew the
hole together. Sew the hole together
by stitching through the front loop of
the 6 sc and pull the yarn. Fasten off.

EARS

· light grey yarn (make 2)
R1: 6 sc in a magic ring = 6 sts
R2: (2i1) x 6 = 12 sts
R3: (1 sc, 2i1) x 6 = 18 sts
R4: (2 sc, 2i1) x 6 = 24 sts
R5: (3 sc, 2i1) x 6 = 30 sts
R6: (4 sc, 2i1) x 6 = 36 sts
R7: (5 sc, 2i1) x 6 = 42 sts
R8: (6 sc, 2i1) x 6 = 48 sts
R9: (7 sc, 2i1) x 6 = 54 sts
R10: (8 sc, 2i1) x 6 = 60 sts
R11-24: sc around = 60 sts

R25: (8 sc, 2»1) x 6 = 54 sts
R26: sc around = 54 sts
R27: (7 sc, 2»1) x 6 = 48 sts
R28: (6 sc, 2»1) x 6 = 42 sts
Finish with a slip stitch. Break the
yarn but leave enough to sew the
ears onto the head.

ARMS

· light grey yarn (make 2)
R1: 6 sc in a magic ring = 6 sts
R2: (2i1) x 6 = 12 sts
R3: (1 sc, 2i1) x 6 = 18 sts
R4-7: sc around = 18 sts
R8: (7 sc, 2»1) x 2 = 16 sts
R9-15: sc around = 16 sts
R16: (6 sc, 2»1) x 2 = 14 sts
R17-30: sc around = 14 sts
Finish with a slip stitch. Break the
yarn but leave enough to sew the
arm onto the body.

CIRCUS HAT

· sea green yarn
R1: 6 sc in a magic ring = 6 sts
R2: (1 sc, 2i1) x 3 = 9 sts
R3-4: sc around = 9 sts
R5: (2 sc, 2i1) x 3 = 12 sts
R6-7: sc around = 12 sts
R8: (3 sc, 2i1) x 3 =15 sts
R9: sc around = 15 sts
R10: (4 sc, 2i1) x 3 = 18 sts
Finish with a slip stitch. Break the
yarn but leave enough to sew the
hat onto the head.

ASSEMBLING

1.
Pin the head to the body to make sure it's placed correctly. The trunk should point downwards. Sew the head and body together. Make sure to stuff the neck properly to keep the head from dangling.

2.
Fold the ears and sew them onto each side of the head. The ears should be placed 2 cm above the neck, and they should bend a little.
See picture A.

3.
Stuff the arms but not all the way to the top. Sew them onto each side of the body, 3 rounds from the neck.

4.
Embroider the eyes and eyelashes on each side of the head with coal grey yarn. Embroider 5 lines on the trunk with coal grey yarn. See picture B.

5.
Cut three long pieces of yarn and sew them on the back of the body, at round 29 from the feet. Make a braid.
See picture C.

6.
Make a pompom for the circus hat. You can find a description for making a pompom on page 16.
Sew the pompom onto the top of the hat. Stuff the hat and sew it onto the head. See picture D.

LITTLE MISS MAGIC

WHAT YOU WILL NEED

MATERIALS - BUNNY
75 g of white cotton
· Drops Safran, color 17

A small amount of grey cotton
· Drops Safran, color 07

A small amount of light pink yarn
· Drops Safran, color 01

2 safety eyes, size 12 mm
Stuffing

2.5-3 mm

MATERIALS - MAGICIAN'S HAT
300 g of black cotton 8/8
· Drops Paris, color 15

4 mm

Cardboard/plastic for the bottom of the hat

ABBREVIATIONS
Chain stitch (ch)
Slip stitch (sl st)
Single crochet (sc)
Increase (2i1)
Decrease (2»1)
Round (R)
Row (RW)

Little Miss Magic will measure approx. 17 cm
in height and 28 cm with her ears stretched.
The magician's hat will measure approx. 20 cm
in height.

THE CUTEST MEMBER OF
LITTLE HAPPY CIRCUS
IS LITTLE MISS MAGIC.
SHE'S A BIT SHY AND HER
FAVOURITE HIDING SPOT IS
INSIDE THE BIG MAGICIAN'S
HAT. HERE SHE CAN HIDE
UNTIL THE SPOTLIGHT
REACHES HER CUTE FACE.

LITTLE MISS MAGIC

HEAD

· white yarn
R1: 6 sc in a magic ring = 6 sts
R2: (2i1) x 6 = 12 sts
R3: (1 sc, 2i1) x 6 = 18 sts
R4: (2 sc, 2i1) x 6 = 24 sts
R5: (3 sc, 2i1) x 6 = 30 sts
R6: (4 sc, 2i1) x 6 = 36 sts
R7: (5 sc, 2i1) x 6 = 42 sts
R8: (6 sc, 2i1) x 6 = 48 sts
R9: (7 sc, 2i1) x 6 = 54 sts
R10: (8 sc, 2i1) x 6 = 60 sts
R11: (9 sc, 2i1) x 6 = 66 sts
R12: (10 sc, 2i1) x 6 = 72 sts
R13: (11 sc, 2i1) x 6 = 78 sts
R14-24: sc around = 78 sts
Insert your safety eyes at this point. They should be placed between rounds 17 and 18 and with 10 sc between them.
R25: (11 sc, 2»1) x 6 = 72 sts
R26: (10 sc, 2»1) x 6 = 66 sts
R27: (9 sc, 2»1) x 6 = 60 sts
R28: (8 sc, 2»1) x 6 = 54 sts
R29: (7 sc, 2»1) x 6 = 48 sts
R30: (6 sc, 2»1) x 6 = 42 sts
R31: (5 sc, 2»1) x 6 = 36 sts
R32: (4 sc, 2»1) x 6 = 30 sts
Finish with a slip stitch and break the yarn.

BODY

· white yarn
R1: 6 sc in a magic ring = 6 sts
R2: (2i1) x 6 = 12 sts
R3: (1 sc, 2i1) x 6 = 18 sts
R4: (2 sc, 2i1) x 6 = 24 sts
R5: (3 sc, 2i1) x 6 = 30 sts
R6: (4 sc, 2i1) x 6 = 36 sts
R7: (5 sc, 2i1) x 6 = 42 sts
R8: (6 sc, 2i1) x 6 = 48 sts
R9: (7 sc, 2i1) x 6 = 54 sts
R10: (8 sc, 2i1) x 6 = 60 sts
R11: (9 sc, 2i1) x 6 = 66 sts
R12-20: sc around = 66 sts
R21: (9 sc, 2»1) x 6 = 60 sts
R22: sc around = 60 sts
R23: (8 sc, 2»1) x 6 = 54 sts
R24: sc around = 54 sts
R25: (7 sc, 2»1) x 6 = 48 sts
R26: sc around = 48 sts
R27: (6 sc, 2»1) x 6 = 42 sts
R28: sc around = 42 sts
R29: (5 sc, 2»1) x 6 = 36 sts
R30: sc around = 36 sts
R31: (4 sc, 2»1) x 6 = 30 sts
Finish with a slip stitch. Break the yarn but leave enough to sew the body and the head together.

EARS

· white yarn (make 2)
R1: 6 sc in a magic ring = 6 sts
R2: (2i1) x 6 = 12 sts
R3: sc around = 12 sts
R4: (1 sc, 2i1) x 6 = 18 sts
R5: sc around = 18 sts
R6: (2 sc, 2i1) x 6 = 24 sts
R7-16: sc around = 24 sts
R17: (10 sc, 2»1) x 2 = 22 sts
R18-20: sc around = 22 sts
R21: (9 sc, 2»1) x 2 = 20 sts
R22-24: sc around = 20 sts
R25: (8 sc, 2»1) x 2 = 18 sts
R26-28: sc around = 18 sts
R29: (7 sc, 2»1) x 2 = 16 sts
R30-39: sc around = 16 sts
Finish with a slip stitch. Break the yarn but leave enough to sew the ear onto the head.

LEGS

· light grey yarn (make 2)
Chain 6 and crochet around these chain stitches. Start in the 2nd chain stitch from the hook.
R1: 4 sc, 3i1, 3 sc, 2i1 = 12 sts
R2: 2i1, 3 sc, 2i1, 1 sc, 2i1, 3 sc, 2i1, 1 sc = 16 sts
R3: 2i1, 5 sc, 2i1, 1 sc, 2i1, 5 sc, 2i1, 1 sc = 20 sts
R4: 2i1, 7 sc, 2i1, 1 sc, 2i1, 7 sc, 2i1, 1 sc = 24 sts
R5: (3 sc, 2i1) x 6 = 30 sts
Change to white yarn.
R6-10: sc around = 30 sts
R11: 13 sc, (2»1) x 3, 11 sc = 27 sts
R12: 9 sc, (1 sc, 2»1) x 3, 9 sc = 24 sts
R13-15: sc around = 24 sts
Finish with a slip stitch. Break the yarn but leave enough to sew the leg onto the body.

ARMS

· white yarn (make 2)
R1: 6 sc in a magic ring = 6 sts
R2: (2i1) x 6 = 12 sts
R3: (1 sc, 2i1) x 6 = 18 sts
R4-7: sc around = 18 sts
R8: (7 sc, 2»1) x 2 = 16 sts
R9: sc around = 16 sts
R10: (6 sc, 2»1) x 2 = 14 sts
R11: sc around = 14 sts
R12: (5 sc, 2»1) x 2 = 12 sts
R13-20: sc around = 12 sts
Finish with a slip stitch. Break the yarn but leave enough to sew the arm onto the body.

TAIL

· white yarn
Make a pompom. See description on page 16.

MAGICIAN'S HAT

· black yarn
R1: 6 sc in a magic ring = 6 sts
R2: (2i1) x 6 = 12 sts
R3: (1 sc, 2i1) x 6 = 18 sts
R4: (2 sc, 2i1) x 6 = 24 sts
R5: (3 sc, 2i1) x 6 = 30 sts
R6: (4 sc, 2i1) x 6 = 36 sts
R7: (5 sc, 2i1) x 6 = 42 sts
R8: (6 sc, 2i1) x 6 = 48 sts
R9: (7 sc, 2i1) x 6 = 54 sts
R10: (8 sc, 2i1) x 6 = 60 sts
R11: (9 sc, 2i1) x 6 = 66 sts
R12: (10 sc, 2i1) x 6 = 72 sts
R13: (11 sc, 2i1) x 6 = 78 sts
R14: (12 sc, 2i1) x 6 = 84 sts
R15: (13 sc, 2i1) x 6 = 90 sts
R16: (14 sc, 2i1) x 6 = 96 sts
R17: (15 sc, 2i1) x 6 = 102 sts
R18: (16 sc, 2i1) x 6 = 108 sts
R19: in the backloop only, sc around = 108 sts
R20-56: sc around = 108 sts
R57: in the front loop only, (17 sc, 2i1) x 6 = 114 sts
R58: (18 sc, 2i1) x 6 = 120 sts
R59: (19 sc, 2i1) x 6 = 126 sts
R60: (20 sc, 2i1) x 6 = 132 sts
R61: (21 sc, 2i1) x 6 = 138 sts
R62: (22 sc, 2i1) x 6 = 144 sts
R63: (23 sc, 2i1) x 6 = 150 sts
Finish with a slip stitch and break the yarn. Fasten off.

ASSEMBLING

1.

Stuff the head and the body and sew them together. Embroider the nose with light pink yarn. See picture A.

2.

Stuff the legs and pin them to the body. Make sure the bunny sits properly before sewing the legs on. I've sewn the legs onto the body between rounds 9 and 11 and with 6 stitches in between them.
See picture B.

3.

Stuff the arms but not all the way to the top. Sew them onto each side of the body at the neck.

4.

Sew the ears onto the head with 11 stitches between them. See picture C.

5.

Sew the tail onto the back of the body. See picture D.

6.

You can put a round circle of cardboard or plastic at the bottom of the magician's hat if you wish to stabilize the bottom.

LITTLE YELLOW LION

WHAT YOU WILL NEED

MATERIALS
110 g of curry yellow cotton
· Drops Loves You 6, color 105

50 g of off-white cotton
· Drops Loves You 6, color 101

6 g of light brown cotton
· Drops Loves You 6, color 104

2 safety eyes, size 6 mm
Stuffing

2.5-3 mm

ABBREVIATIONS
Chain stitch (ch)
Slip stitch (sl st)
Single crochet (sc)
Double treble crochet (dtr)
- See page 18.
Increase (2i1)
Decrease (2»1)
Round (R)

Little Yellow Lion will measure approx. 40 cm in height.

NO NEED TO WORRY - THERE'S NO DANGER AHEAD. LITTLE YELLOW LION IS A GENTLE GUY. HE'S JUST AS CUDDLY AS A PET CAT AND IF IT WAS UP TO HIM, HE'D BE SCRATCHED BEHIND HIS EARS ALL DAY LONG.

LITTLE YELLOW LION

LEGS

· curry yellow yarn (make 2)
Stuff as you go!
R1: 6 sc in a magic ring = 6 sts
R2: (2i1) x 6 = 12 sts
R3: (3 sc, 2i1) x 3 = 15 sts
R4-7: sc around = 15 sts
R8: (4 sc, 2i1) x 3 = 18 sts
R9-12: sc around = 18 sts
R13: (2 sc, 2i1) x 6 = 24 sts
R14-15: sc around = 24 sts
Finish with a slip stitch. Break
the yarn and crochet the other
leg. Don't break the yarn on the
2nd leg but continue crocheting
the body.

BODY

· curry yellow yarn
Chain 5 and insert your hook in any
stitch on the first leg.
Crochet around that leg and continue
crocheting around both the chain
stitches and the legs. You can find
a description on page 20 on how to
join legs.
R16: 24 sc, 1 sc in each of the 5 chain
stitches, 24 sc, 1 sc in each of the 5
chain stitches = 58 sts
R17: (28 sc, 2i1) x 2 = 60 sts

R18: (9 sc, 2i1) x 6 = 66 sts
R19: (10 sc, 2i1) x 6 = 72 sts
R20: (11 sc, 2i1) x 6 = 78 sts
R21: (12 sc, 2i1) x 6 = 84 sts
R22-31: sc around = 84 sts
R32: (12 sc, 2»1) x 6 = 78 sts
R33-34: sc around = 78 sts
R35: (11 sc, 2»1) x 6 = 72 sts
R36-37: sc around = 72 sts
R38: (10 sc, 2»1) x 6 = 66 sts
R39-40: sc around = 66 sts
R41: (9 sc, 2»1) x 6 = 60 sts
R42-43: sc around = 60 sts
R44: (8 sc, 2»1) x 6 = 54 sts
R45-47: sc around = 54 sts
R48: (7 sc, 2»1) x 6 = 48 sts
R49-51: sc around = 48 sts
R52: (6 sc, 2»1) x 6 = 42 sts
R53-55: sc around = 42 sts
R56: (5 sc, 2»1) x 6 = 36 sts
R57-59: sc around = 36 sts
R60: (4 sc, 2»1) x 6 = 30 sts
R61-63: sc around = 30 sts
R64: (3 sc, 2»1) x 6 = 24 sts
R65-66: sc around = 24 sts
Finish with a slip stitch. Break
the yarn but leave enough
to sew the body and the
head together.

HEAD

· off-white yarn
R1: 6 sc in a magic ring = 6 sts
R2: (2i1) x 6 = 12 sts
R3: (1 sc, 2i1) x 6 = 18 sts
R4: (2 sc, 2i1) x 6 = 24 sts
R5: (3 sc, 2i1) x 6 = 30 sts
R6: (4 sc, 2i1) x 6 = 36 sts
R7: (5 sc, 2i1) x 6 = 42 sts
R8: (6 sc, 2i1) x 6 = 48 sts
R9: (7 sc, 2i1) x 6 = 54 sts
R10: (8 sc, 2i1) x 6 = 60 sts
R11: (9 sc, 2i1) x 6 = 66 sts
R12: (10 sc, 2i1) x 6 = 72 sts
R13-24: sc around = 72 sts
Insert your safety eyes at this
point. They should be placed
between rounds 14 and 15 and
with 5 sc between them.
R25: (10 sc, 2»1) x 6 = 66 sts
R26: (9 sc, 2»1) x 6 = 60 sts
R27: (8 sc, 2»1) x 6 = 54 sts
R28: (7 sc, 2»1) x 6 = 48 sts
R29: (6 sc, 2»1) x 6 = 42 sts
R30: (5 sc, 2»1) x 6 = 36 sts
R31: (4 sc, 2»1) x 6 = 30 sts
R32: (3 sc, 2»1) x 6 = 24 sts
Finish with a slip stitch and break
the yarn.

MUZZLE

· off-white yarn
R1: 6 sc in a magic ring = 6 sts
R2: (2i1) x 6 = 12 sts
R3: (1 sc, 2i1) x 6 = 18 sts
R4: (2 sc, 2i1) x 6 = 24 sts
R5: (3 sc, 2i1) x 6 = 30 sts
R6: (4 sc, 2i1) x 6 = 36 sts
R7-11: sc around = 36 sts
Finish with a slip stitch. Break
the yarn but leave enough to
sew the muzzle onto the head.

NOSE

· light brown yarn
R1: 6 sc in a magic ring = 6 sts
R2: (1 sc, 2i1) x 3 = 9 sts
R3: (2 sc, 2i1) x 3 = 12 sts
R4: (3 sc, 2i1) x 3 = 15 sts
R5: sc around = 15 sts
R6: (4 sc, 2i1) x 3 = 18 sts
Change to off-white yarn
R7-13: sc around = 18 sts
Finish with a slip stitch. Break
the yarn but leave enough to
sew the nose onto the muzzle.

EARS

· off-white yarn (make 2)
R1: 6 sc in a magic ring = 6 sts
R2: (2i1) x 6 = 12 sts
R3: sc around = 12 sts
R4: (1 sc, 2i1) x 6 = 18 sts

R5: sc around = 18 sts
R6: (2 sc, 2i1) x 6 = 24 sts
R7-9: sc around = 24 sts
Finish with a slip stitch. Break
the yarn but leave enough to
sew the ear onto the head.

MANE

· curry yellow yarn
R1: 6 sc in a magic ring = 6 sts
R2: (2i1) x 6 = 12 sts
R3: (1 sc, 2i1) x 6 = 18 sts
R4: (2 sc, 2i1) x 6 = 24 sts
R5: (3 sc, 2i1) x 6 = 30 sts
R6: (4 sc, 2i1) x 6 = 36 sts
R7: (5 sc, 2i1) x 6 = 42 sts
R8: (6 sc, 2i1) x 6 = 48 sts
R9: (7 sc, 2i1) x 6 = 54 sts
R10: (8 sc, 2i1) x 6 = 60 sts
R11: (9 sc, 2i1) x 6 = 66 sts
R12-15: sc around = 66 sts
R16: (1 sc, 1 dtr) x 33 =
66 sts
R17: sc around = 66 sts
R18: (1 sc, 1 dtr) x 33 =
66 sts
R19: sc around = 66 sts
R20: (1 sc, 1 dtr) x 33 =
66 sts
R21: sc around = 66 sts
R22: (1 sc, 1 dtr) x 33 = 66 sts
R23: sc around = 66 sts
Finish with a slip stitch. Break the
yarn but leave enough to sew the
hat onto the head.

ARMS

· off-white yarn (make 2)
R1: 6 sc in a magic ring = 6 sts
R2: (2i1) x 6 = 12 sts
R3: (2 sc, 2i1) x 4 = 16 sts
R4-6: sc around = 16 sts
Change to curry yellow yarn
R7-24: sc around = 16 sts
R25: (6 sc, 2»1) x 2 = 14 sts
R26-28: sc around = 14 sts
Finish with a slip stitch. Break
the yarn but leave enough to
sew the arm onto the body.

TAIL

· light brown yarn
Stuff as you go but only the tip of
the tail!
R1: 6 sc in a magic ring = 6 sts
R2: 2i1, 5 sc = 7 sts
R3: 2i1, 6 sc = 8 sts
R4: 2i1, 7 sc = 9 sts
R5: 2i1, 8 sc = 10 sts
R6: 2i1, 9 sc = 11 sts
R7: 2i1, 10 sc = 12 sts
R8: (3 sc, 2i1) x 3 = 15 sts
R9: sc around = 15 sts
R10: (3 sc, 2»1) x 3 = 12 sts
R11: (2 sc, 2»1) x 3 = 9 sts
Change to curry yellow yarn
R12-39: sc around = 9 sts
Finish with a slip stitch. Break
the yarn but leave enough to
sew the tail onto the body.

ASSEMBLING

1.

Pin the nose to the muzzle and sew it on along the edge. Thread a needle with light brown yarn and attach the tip of the nose. Embroider a mouth. See picture A.

2.

Stuff the head and the muzzle. Pin the muzzle to the head, 3 rounds below the eyes. Sew the muzzle all the way around. See picture B.

3.

Place the mane onto the head and sew it all the way around. Sew the head and body together. Make sure to stuff the neck properly to keep the head from dangling.

4.

Stuff the arms but not all the way to the top. Sew them onto to each side of the body at the neck.

A

B

5.

Fold the ears and sew them onto the top of the head. They should be placed just behind the "knots" and with 6 stitches between them. See picture C.

6.

Sew the tail onto the back of the body, at round 29 from the feet. See picture D.

C

D

LITTLE
YELLOW LION

CLOWN OF THE DAY

WHAT YOU WILL NEED

MATERIALS

14 g of grey cotton
· Drops Safran, color 07

30 g of dark blue cotton
· Drops Safran, color 09

25 g of off-white cotton
· Drops Safran, color 18

30 g of curry yellow cotton
· Drops Loves You 6, color 105

10 g of white cotton
· Drops Safran, color 17

A small amount of petrol blue cotton
· Drops Safran, color 51

A small amount of black cotton
· Drops Safran, color 16

Stuffing

2.5-3 mm

ABBREVIATIONS

Chain stitch (ch)
Slip stitch (sl st)
Single crochet (sc)
Increase (2i1)
Decrease (2»1)
Round (R)

Clown of The Day will measure
approx. 35 cm in height.

CLOWN OF THE DAY
HAS ALWAYS KNOWN
THAT HE WANTED TO BE
A CLOWN. AT CLOWN
SCHOOL HE QUICKLY
LEARNED THAT HIS BLUE
NOSE IS SOMETHING
COMPLETELY UNIQUE AND
HE WEARS IT WITH PRIDE.

CLOWN OF THE DAY

LEGS

· grey yarn (make 2)

Stuff as you go!

R1: 6 sc in a magic ring = 6 sts
R2: (2i1) x 6 = 12 sts
R3: sc around = 12 sts
R4: (5 sc, 2i1) x 2 = 14 sts
R5-7: sc around = 14 sts
R8: (6 sc, 2i1) x 2 = 16 sts
R9-11: sc around = 16 sts
R12: (7 sc, 2i1) x 2 = 18 sts
R13-23: sc around = 18 sts
Finish with a slip stitch. Break the yarn and crochet the other leg. Don't break the yarn on the 2nd leg but continue crocheting the body.

BODY

· grey yarn

Chain 9 and insert your hook in any stitch on the first leg.
Crochet around that leg and continue by crocheting around both the chain stitches and the legs. You can find a description on page 20 on how to join legs.
R24: 18 sc, 1 sc in each of the 9 chain stitches, 18 sc, 1 sc in each of the 9 chain stitches = 54 sts

R25: sc around = 54 sts
R26: (8 sc, 2i1) x 6 = 60 sts
R27: sc around = 60 sts
R28: (9 sc, 2i1) x 6 = 66 sts
R29-31: sc around = 66 sts
Change to dark blue yarn
R32-38: sc around = 66 sts
R39: (9 sc, 2»1) x 6 = 60 sts
R40-42: sc around = 60 sts
R43: (8 sc, 2»1) x 6 = 54 sts
R44-46: sc around = 54 sts
R47: (7 sc, 2»1) x 6 = 48 sts
R48-50: sc around = 48 sts
R51: (6 sc, 2»1) x 6 = 42 sts
R52-54: sc around = 42 sts
R55: (5 sc, 2»1) x 6 = 36 sts
R56-58: sc around = 36 sts
R59: (4 sc, 2»1) x 6 = 30 sts
R60-62: sc around = 30 sts
Finish with a slip stitch. Break the yarn but leave enough to sew the body and the head together.

HEAD

· off-white yarn

R1: 6 sc in a magic ring = 6 sts
R2: (2i1) x 6 = 12 sts
R3: (1 sc, 2i1) x 6 = 18 sts
R4: (2 sc, 2i1) x 6 = 24 sts
R5: (3 sc, 2i1) x 6 = 30 sts

R6: (4 sc, 2i1) x 6 = 36 sts
R7: (5 sc, 2i1) x 6 = 42 sts
R8: (6 sc, 2i1) x 6 = 48 sts
R9: (7 sc, 2i1) x 6 = 54 sts
R10: (8 sc, 2i1) x 6 = 60 sts
R11: (9 sc, 2i1) x 6 = 66 sts
R12: (10 sc, 2i1) x 6 = 72 sts
R13-25: sc around = 72 sts
R26: (10 sc, 2»1) x 6 = 66 sts
R27: (9 sc, 2»1) x 6 = 60 sts
R28: (8 sc, 2»1) x 6 = 54 sts
R29: (7 sc, 2»1) x 6 = 48 sts
R30: (6 sc, 2»1) x 6 = 42 sts
R31: (5 sc, 2»1) x 6 = 36 sts
R32: (4 sc, 2»1) x 6 = 30 sts
Finish with a slip stitch and break the yarn.

ARMS

· off-white yarn (make 2)

Stuff as you go!

R1: 6 sc in a magic ring = 6 sts
R2: (2i1) x 6 = 12 sts
R3-6: sc around = 12 sts
Change to dark blue yarn
R7-41: sc around = 12 sts
Finish with a slip stitch. Break the yarn but leave enough to sew the arm onto the body.

NOSE

· petrol blue

R1: 6 sc in a magic ring = 6 sts
R2: (2i1) x 6 = 12 sts
R3: (1 sc, 2i1) x 6 = 18 sts
R4: (2 sc, 2i1) x 6 = 24 sts
R5: (3 sc, 2i1) x 6 = 30 sts
R6-9: sc around = 30 sts
R10: (3 sc, 2»1) x 6 = 24 sts
Finish with a slip stitch. Break the yarn but leave enough to sew the nose onto the head.

HAIR

· curry yellow yarn (make 2)
Stuff as you go!
R1: 6 sc in a magic ring = 6 sts
R2: (2i1) x 6 = 12 sts
R3-5: sc around = 12 sts
R6: (1 sc, 2i1) x 6 = 18 sts
R7: (2 sc, 2i1) x 6 = 24 sts
R8-11: sc around = 24 sts
R12: (2 sc, 2»1) x 6 = 18 sts
R13: (2 sc, 2i1) x 6 = 24 sts
R14: (3 sc, 2i1) x 6 = 30 sts
R15: (4 sc, 2i1) x 6 = 36 sts
R16-17: sc around = 36 sts
R18: (4 sc, 2»1) x 6 = 30 sts
R19: (3 sc, 2»1) x 6 = 24 sts
R20: (3 sc, 2i1) x 6 = 30 sts
R21: (4 sc, 2i1) x 6 = 36 sts

R22: (5 sc, 2i1) x 6 = 42 sts
R23-29: sc around = 42 sts
R30: (5 sc, 2»1) x 6 = 36 sts
R31: (4 sc, 2»1) x 6 = 30 sts
Finish with a slip stitch. Break the yarn but leave enough to sew the hair onto the head.

SUSPENDERS

· black yarn (make 4)
R1: 6 sc in a magic ring = 6 sts
Finish with a slip stitch. Break the yarn but leave enough to sew the suspender onto the body.
Don't break the yarn on two of the circles but continue making the strap.
Chain 50 and sew the strap onto the other circle. Make sure that your row of chain stitches fits your clown. You might have to crochet a few more or less chain stitches.

SWIMMING RING

· white yarn
Chain 18 and join to the 1st chain forming a ring.
R1-4: sc around = 18 sts
Change to bordeaux red yarn
R5-9: sc around = 18 sts
Change to white yarn
R10-14: sc around = 18 sts
Continue by changing between red and white stripes until the swimming ring has 21 stripes in total.
Make each stripe 5 rounds except on the first and last stripe.
The last stripe consists of only 1 round of white to make the most invisible seam.
Finish with a slip stitch but leave enough to sew the ends together.

ASSEMBLING

1.
Stuff the head. Embroider 2 crosses as eyes. They should be placed from round 13 to round 16 and with 4 sc between them. Stuff the nose and sew it on below the eyes. See picture A.

2.
Stuff the hair pieces. Pin them to the head to make sure they are placed correctly. Sew them on 6 rounds from the top. See picture B.

3.
Sew the head and the body together. Make sure to stuff the neck properly to keep the head from dangling.

4.
Stuff the arms but not all the way to the top. Sew them onto each side of the body by the neck.

5.
It's now time to attach the suspenders. Sew the button on, right where the pants change to the color blue. Let the row of chain stitches stretch over the shoulder and sew the other button on at the back of the body. Please make sure the row of chain stitches don't twist. See picture C.

6.
Stuff the swimming ring but not too tightly. Sew the swimming ring together at the ends and put it on the clown. See picture D.

MR. STRONG

WHAT YOU WILL NEED

MATERIALS

65 g of off-white cotton
· Drops Safran, color 18

35 g of bordeaux cotton
· Drops Loves You 6, color 110

30 g of black cotton
· Drops Safran, color 16

7 g of grey cotton
· Drops Safran, color 07

Stuffing
Black sewing thread

2.5-
3 mm

ABBREVIATIONS

Chain stitch (ch)
Slip stitch (sl st)
Single crochet (sc)
Half double crochet (hdc)
Double crochet (dc)
Increase (2i1)
Decrease (2»1)
Round (R)
Row (RW)

Mr. Strong will measure
approx. 30 cm in height.

BEING THE STRONG MAN
OF A CIRCUS IS NOT
JUST LIFTING WEIGHTS
AND BEING TOUGH. EVERY
TIME LITTLE HAPPY
CIRCUS ARRIVES AT A
NEW TOWN, MR. STRONG
HELPS TO RAISE THE
BIG CIRCUS TENT.

MR. STRONG

LEGS
· off-white yarn (make 2)
Stuff as you go!
R1: 6 sc in a magic ring = 6 sts
R2: (2i1) x 6 = 12 sts
R3: (1 sc, 2i1) x 6 = 18 sts
R4-19: sc around = 18 sts
Finish with a slip stitch. Break the yarn and crochet the other leg. Don't break the yarn on the 2nd leg but continue crocheting the body.

BODY
· off-white yarn
Chain 15 and insert your hook in any stitch on the first leg. Crochet around that leg and continue by crocheting around both the chain stitches and the legs. You can find a description on page 20 on how to join legs.

R20: 18 sc, 1 sc in each of the 15 chain stitches, 18 sc, 1 sc in each of the 15 chain stitches = 66 sts
R21-40: sc around = 66 sts
R41: (9 sc, 2»1) = 60 sts
R42-43: sc around = 60 sts
R44: (8 sc, 2»1) x 6 = 54 sts
R45-46: sc around = 54 sts
R47: (7 sc, 2»1) x 6 = 48 sts
R48-49: sc around = 48 sts
R50: (6 sc, 2»1) x 6 = 42 sts
R51-52: sc around = 42 sts
R53: (5 sc, 2»1) x 6 = 36 sts
R54-56: sc around = 36 sts
R57: (4 sc, 2»1) x 6 = 30 sts
R58-60: sc around = 30 sts
Finish with a slip stitch. Break the yarn but leave enough to sew the body and the head together.

HEAD
· off-white yarn
R1: 6 sc in a magic ring = 6 sts
R2: (2i1) x 6 = 12 sts
R3: (1 sc, 2i1) x 6 = 18 sts
R4: (2 sc, 2i1) x 6 = 24 sts
R5: (3 sc, 2i1) x 6 = 30 sts
R6: (4 sc, 2i1) x 6 = 36 sts
R7: (5 sc, 2i1) x 6 = 42 sts
R8: (6 sc, 2i1) x 6 = 48 sts
R9: (7 sc, 2i1) x 6 = 54 sts
R10: (8 sc, 2i1) x 6 = 60 sts
R11: (9 sc, 2i1) x 6 = 66 sts
R12-22: sc around = 66 sts
R23: (9 sc, 2»1) x 6 = 60 sts
R24: (8 sc, 2»1) x 6 = 54 sts
R25: (7 sc, 2»1) x 6 = 48 sts
R26: (6 sc, 2»1) x 6 = 42 sts
R27: (5 sc, 2»1) x 6 = 36 sts
R28: (4 sc, 2»1) x 6 = 30 sts
Finish with a slip stitch and break the yarn.

HAIR
· black yarn
R1: 6 sc in a magic ring = 6 sts
R2: (2i1) x 6 = 12 sts
R3: (1 sc, 2i1) x 6 = 18 sts
R4: (2 sc, 2i1) x 6 = 24 sts
R5: (3 sc, 2i1) x 6 = 30 sts
R6: (4 sc, 2i1) x 6 = 36 sts
R7: (5 sc, 2i1) x 6 = 42 sts
R8: (6 sc, 2i1) x 6 = 48 sts
R9: (7 sc, 2i1) x 6 = 54 sts
R10: (8 sc, 2i1) x 6 = 60 sts
R11: (9 sc, 2i1) x 6 = 66 sts
R12-17: sc around = 66 sts
R18: 1 sc, 8 hdc, 34 sc, 22 hdc, 1 sl st = 66 sts
R19: 1 sc, 8 hdc, 33 sc, 23 hdc, 1 sl st = 66 sts
Finish with a slip stitch. Break the yarn but leave enough to sew the hair onto the head.

ARMS
· off-white (make 2)
R1: 6 sc in a magic ring = 6 sts
R2: (2i1) x 6 = 12 sts
R3-41: sc around = 12 sts
Finish with a slip stitch. Break the yarn but leave enough to sew the arm onto the body.

MOUSTACHE
· black yarn (make 2)
R1: 6 sc in a magic ring = 6 sts
R2: sc around = 6 sts
R3: 2i1, 5 sc = 7 sts
R4-5: sc around = 7 sts
R6: 2i1, 6 sc = 8 sts
R7: sc around = 8 sts
R8: 2i1, 7 sc = 9 sts
R9: sc around = 9 sts
R10: 2i1, 8 sc = 10 sts
R11: (2»1) x 5 = 5 sts
Finish with a slip stitch. Break the yarn but leave enough to sew the moustache together and onto the head.

SUIT
TROUSERS
· bordeaux red yarn (make 2)
Chain 19 and assemble to a ring.
R1-5: sc around = 19 sts

Finish with a slip stitch. Break the yarn and crochet the other trouser. Don't break the yarn on the 2nd trouser but continue crocheting the suit.

SUIT

· bordeaux red yarn
Chain 15 and insert your hook into any stitch on the first leg. Crochet around that leg and continue by crocheting around both the chain stitches and the trousers. You can find a description on page 20 on how to join legs.
R6: 19 sc, 1 sc in each of the 15 chain stitches, 19 sc, 1 sc in each of the 15 chain stitches = 68 sts
R7-26: sc around = 68 sts
R27: (9 sc, 2»1) x 6, 2 sc = 62 sts
Now it's time to crochet in rows. Turn each row with a chain stitch.
Continue with the back of the suit.

SUIT
BACK

· bordeaux red yarn
Rw28: 1 sc in each of the next 6 sts = 6 sts
Rw29: 1 sc in each of the next 21 sts = 21 sts
Rw30: 2»1, 17 sc, 2»1 = 19 sts
Rw31: sc across = 19 sts
Rw32: 2»1, 15 sc, 2»1 = 17 sts
Rw33: sc across = 17 sts
Rw34: 2»1, 13 sc, 2»1 = 15 sts
Rw35: 2»1, 11 sc, 2»1 = 13 sts
Rw36: 2»1, 9 sc, 2»1 = 11 sts
Rw37: sc across = 11 sts
Rw38: 2 dc, 1 hdc, 5 sc, 1 hdc, 2 dc = 11 sts
Break the yarn and fasten off.

SUIT
STRAP

· bordeaux red yarn
Begin in the 12th sc from the back of the suit.
Rw1: 1 sc in each of the next 9 sc = 9 sts
Rw2: 2»1, 7 sc = 8 sts
Rw3: sc across = 8 sts
Rw4: 2»1, 6 sc = 7 sts
Rw5: sc across = 7 sts
Rw6: 2»1, 5 sc = 6 sts
Rw7: sc across = 6 sts
Rw8: 2»1, 4 sc = 5 sts
Rw9: sc across = 5 sts
Rw10: 2»1, 3 sc = 4 sts
Rw11: sc across = 4 sts
Rw12: 2»1, 2 sc = 3 sts
Rw13: sc across = 3 sts
Rw14: 2»1, 1 sc = 2 sts
Rw15-26: sc across = 2 sts
Rw27: 1 sc, 2i1 = 3 sts
Break the yarn but leave enough to sew the strap onto the back of the suit.

SUIT
SECOND STRAP

· bordeaux red yarn
Begin in the 2nd sc from the first strap.
Rw1: 1 sc in each of the next 9 sts = 9 sts
Rw2: 7 sc, 2»1 = 8 sts
Rw3: sc across = 8 sts
Rw4: 6 sc, 2»1 = 7 sts
Rw5: sc across = 7 sts
Rw6: 5 sc, 2»1 = 6 sts
Rw7: sc across = 6 sts
Rw8: 4 sc, 2»1 = 5 sts
Rw9: sc across = 5 sts
Rw10: 3 sc, 2»1 = 4 sts
Rw11: sc across = 4 sts
Rw12: 2 sc, 2»1 = 3 sts
Rw13: sc across = 3 sts
Rw14: 1 sc, 2»1 = 2 sts
Rw15-26: sc across = 2 sts
Rw27: 2i1, 1 sc = 3 sts
Break the yarn but leave enough to sew the strap onto the back of the suit. Sew the two straps and the back piece together and crochet a line of slip stitches all the way around the neck opening and the two armholes.

WEIGHT BAR

· black yarn
Stuff as you go!
R1: 6 sc in a magic ring = 6 sts
R2: (2i1) x 6 = 12 sts
R3: (1 sc, 2i1) x 6 = 18 sts
R4: (2 sc, 2i1) x 6 = 24 sts
R5: (3 sc, 2i1) x 6 = 30 sts
R6: (4 sc, 2i1) x 6 = 36 sts
R7-12: sc around = 36 sts
R13: (4 sc, 2»1) x 6 = 30 sts
R14: (3 sc, 2»1) x 6 = 24 sts
R15: (2 sc, 2»1) x 6 = 18 sts
R16: (1 sc, 2»1) x 6 = 12 sts
Change to grey yarn
R17-49: sc around = 12 sts
Change to black yarn
R50: (1 sc, 2i1) x 6 = 18 sts
R51: (2 sc, 2i1) x 6 = 24 sts
R52: (3 sc, 2i1) x 6 = 30 sts
R53: (4 sc, 2i1) x 6 = 36 sts
R54-60: sc around = 36 sts
R61: (4 sc, 2»1) x 6 = 30 sts
R62: (3 sc, 2»1) x 6 = 24 sts
R63: (2 sc, 2»1) x 6 = 18 sts
R64: (1 sc, 2»1) x 6 = 12 sts
R65: (2»1) x 6 = 6 sts
Finish with a slip stitch. Break the yarn but leave enough to sew the hole together. Sew the hole together by stitching through the front loop of the 6 sc and pull the yarn. Fasten off.

ASSEMBLING

1.
Stuff the head and sew the head and the body together. Make sure to stuff the neck properly to keep the head from dangling. Place the hair so he gets a side parting, and sew all the way around.

2.
Sew the moustache together at the middle and sew it onto the head. It should be placed between rounds 8 and 10 from the eyes. See picture A.

3.
Stuff the arms but not all the way to the top. Sew them onto each side of the body, 1 round below the neck.

4.
It's now time to make the chest hair. Thread a needle with black sewing thread and sew small pieces of thread around the chest. Cut the threads to make it look like small strings of hair. See picture B.

5.
Sew in the ends of the suit. See picture C.

6.
Dress Mr. Strong with his suit.

MR. STRONG

WALTER THE WALRUS

WHAT YOU WILL NEED

MATERIALS
85 g of light brown cotton
· Drops Safran, color 22

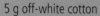 2.5-3 mm

5 g off-white cotton
· Drops Safran, color 17

A scrap of beige cotton
· Drops Safran, color 18

A small amount of ice blue cotton
· Drops Safran, color 50

A small amount of of petrol blue cotton
· Drops Safran, 51

2 safety eyes, size 6 mm
Stuffing

ABBREVIATIONS
Chain stitch (ch)
Slip stitch (sl st)
Single crochet (sc)
Increase (2i1)
Decrease (2»1)
Round (R)

Walter the Walrus will measure
approx. 30 cm in length.

WHEN WALTER THE WALRUS ENTERS THE CIRCUS ARENA, EVERY PERSON IN THE AUDIENCE IS IMPRESSED BY HIS MANY TALENTS, WHICH INCLUDE JUGGLING, DANCING, CLAPPING AND CATCHING BALLS.

WALTER THE WALRUS

FINS

· light brown yarn (make 2)
R1: 6 sc in a magic ring = 6 sts
R2: (2i1) x 6 = 12 sts
R3: sc around = 12 sts
R4: (1 sc, 2i1) x 6 = 18 sts
R5-14: sc around = 18 sts
Finish with a slip stitch. Break the yarn and crochet the other fin. Don't break the yarn on the 2nd fin but continue crocheting the body.

BODY

· light brown yarn
Stuff as you go!
Chain 6 and insert your hook in any stitch on the first leg.
Crochet around that leg and continue by crocheting around both the chain stitches and the legs. You can find a description on page 20 on how to join legs.
R15: 18 sc, 1 sc in each of the 6 chain stitches, 18 sc, 1 sc in each of the 6 chain stitches = 48 sts
R16-22: sc around = 48 sts
R23: (7 sc, 2i1) x 6 = 54 sts
R24-26: sc around = 54 sts
R27: (8 sc, 2i1) x 6 = 60 sts
R28-30: sc around = 60 sts
R31: (9 sc, 2i1) x 6 = 66 sts
R32-33: sc around = 66 sts
R34: (10 sc, 2i1) x 6 = 72 sts
R35-36: sc around = 72 sts
R37: (11 sc, 2i1) x 6 = 78 sts
R38-39: sc around = 78 sts
R40: (12 sc, 2i1) x 6 = 84 sts
R41-42: sc around = 84 sts
R43: (13 sc, 2i1) x 6 = 90 sts
R44-66: sc around = 90 sts
R67: (13 sc, 2»1) x 6 = 84 sts
R68: sc around = 84 sts
R69: (12 sc, 2»1) x 6 = 78 sts
R70: sc around = 78 sts
R71: (11 sc, 2»1) x 6 = 72 sts
R72: (10 sc, 2»1) x 6 = 66 sts
R73: (9 sc, 2»1) x 6 = 60 sts
R74: (8 sc, 2»1) x 6 = 54 sts
R75: (7 sc, 2»1) x 6 = 48 sts
R76: (6 sc, 2»1) x 6 = 42 sts
R77: (5 sc, 2»1) x 6 = 36 sts
R78: (4 sc, 2»1) x 6 = 30 sts
R79: (3 sc, 2»1) x 6 = 24 sts
R80: (2 sc, 2»1) x 6 = 18 sts
R81: (1 sc, 2»1) x 6 = 12 sts
R82: (2»1) x 6 = 6 sts
Finish with a slip stitch. Break the yarn but leave enough to sew the hole together. Sew the hole together by stitching through the front loop of the 6 sc and pull the yarn. Fasten off.

MUZZLE

· light brown yarn
R1: 6 sc in a magic ring = 6 sts
R2: (2i1) x 6 = 12 sts
R3: (1 sc, 2i1) x 6 = 18 sts
R4: (2 sc, 2i1) x 6 = 24 sts
R5: (3 sc, 2i1) x 6 = 30 sts
R6: (4 sc, 2i1) x 6 = 36 sts
R7: (5 sc, 2i1) x 6 = 42 sts
R8: (6 sc, 2i1) x 6 = 48 sts
R9: (7 sc, 2i1) x 6 = 54 sts
R10-15: sc around = 54 sts
Finish with a slip stitch. Break the yarn but leave enough to sew the muzzle onto the head.

TUSKS

· white yarn (make 2)
R1: 6 sc in a magic ring = 6 sts
R2: sc around = 6 sts
R3: 2i1, 5 sc = 7 sts
R4: sc around = 7 sts
R5: 2i1, 6 sc = 8 sts
R6: sc around = 8 sts
R7: 2i1, 7 sc = 9 sts
R8-12: sc around = 9 sts
Finish with a slip stitch. Break the yarn but leave enough to sew the tusk on below the muzzle.

EYES

· white yarn (make 2)
R1: 6 sc in a magic ring = 6 sts
R2: (2i1) x 6 = 12 sts
R3: (1 sc, 2i1) x 6 = 18 sts
R4-5: sc around = 18 sts
Insert your safety eyes at this point. They should be placed in the centre of the eye.
R6: (1 sc, 2»1) x 6 = 12 sts
Finish with a slip stitch. Break the yarn but leave enough to sew the eye onto the head.

FRONT FLIPPERS

· light brown yarn (make 2)
R1: 6 sc in a magic ring = 6 sts
R2: (2i1) x 6 = 12 sts
R3: (1 sc, 2i1) x 6 = 18 sts
R4: (2 sc, 2i1) x 6 = 24 sts
R5: (3 sc, 2i1) x 6 = 30 sts
R6-9: sc around = 30 sts
R10: (3 sc, 2»1) x 6 = 24 sts
R11-17: sc around = 24 sts
Finish with a slip stitch. Break the yarn but leave enough to sew the front flipper onto the body.

FISH

· light grey yarn
Stuff as you go!
R1: 6 sc in a magic ring = 6 sts
R2: (2i1) x 6 = 12 sts
R3: (1 sc, 2i1) x 6 = 18 sts
R4-9: sc around = 18 sts
Insert your safety eyes at this point. They should be placed on each side and between rounds 5 and 6.
R10: (1 sc, 2»1) x 6 = 12 sts
R11-12: sc around = 12 sts
Fold the fish, crochet the edge together and continue by crocheting in rows.
Rw13: sc across = 6 sts, turn with two chain stitches
Rw14: (in the same stitch, 1 dc, 1 sc) x 6 = 12 sts
Break the yarn and fasten off.

BALL

· ice blue yarn
Stuff as you go!
R1: 6 sc in a magic ring = 6 sts
R2: (2i1) x 6 = 12 sts
Change to petrol blue yarn
R3: (1 sc, 2i1) x 6 = 18 sts
R4: (2 sc, 2i1) x 6 = 24 sts
Change to ice blue yarn
R5: (3 sc, 2i1) x 6 = 30 sts
R6: (4 sc, 2i1) x 6 = 36 sts
Change to petrol blue yarn
R7: (5sc, 2i1) x 6 = 42 sts
R8: sc around = 42 sts
Change to ice blue yarn
R9-10: sc around = 42 sts
Change to petrol blue yarn
R11-12: sc around = 42 sts
Change to ice blue yarn
R13-14: sc around = 42 sts
Change to petrol blue yarn
R15: (5 sc, 2»1) x 6 = 36 sts
R16: (4 sc, 2»1) x 6 = 30 sts
Change to ice blue yarn
R17: (3 sc, 2»1) x 6 = 24 sts
R18: (2 sc, 2»1) x 6 = 18 sts
Change to petrol blue yarn
R19: (1 sc, 2»1) x 6 = 12 sts
R20: (2»1) x 6 = 6 sts
Finish with a slip stitch. Break the yarn but leave enough to sew the hole together. Sew the hole together by stitching through the front loop of the 6 sc and pull the yarn. Fasten off.

ASSEMBLING

1.

Pin the muzzle to the head to make sure it's placed correctly and sew it on. Stuff the muzzle before sewing all the way around.
See picture A.

2.

Sew the eyes on, just above the muzzle. The eyes should be attached so closely that they touch each other.
Don't stuff the eyes.
See picture B.

3.

Stuff the tusks, tweezers might be handy. Sew them onto the lower side of the muzzle with 5 sc between them. Cut 20 pieces of beige yarn for the beard. They should be approx. 15 cm long. Divide the pieces of yarn into 2 groups. Sew or crochet 10 pieces of yarn on, in front of each tusk. See picture C.
Stuff the front flippers and pin them to each side of the body.

4.

They should be placed 6 rounds from the muzzle. Before sewing them on, please make sure that your walrus can stand, resting on the flippers.
Make sure to stuff them a bit more before sewing all the way around. See picture D.

WALTER THE
WALRUS

GARLAND

WHAT YOU WILL NEED

MATERIALS

6 g of curry yellow cotton
· Drops Loves You 6, color 105

 2.5-3 mm

6 g of coral cotton
· Drops Loves You 6, color 109

6 g of sea green cotton
· Drops Loves You 6, color 112

6 g of light grey cotton
· Drops Loves You 6, color 103

6 g of coal grey cotton
· Drops Loves You 6, color 118

A small amount of off-white cotton
· Drops Loves You 6, color 101

OR

6 g of light pink cotton
· Drops Safran, color 01

6 g of pink cotton
· Drops Safran, color 02

6 g of coral cotton
· Drops Safran, color 13

6 g of ice blue cotton
· Drops Safran, color 50

6 g of petrol blue cotton
· Drops Safran, color 51

A small amount of off-white cotton
· Drops Safran, color 18

ABBREVIATIONS

Chain stitch (ch)
Slip stitch (sl st)
Single crochet (sc)
Decrease (2»1)
Row (RW)

GARLAND

The garland is crocheted in rows. Each row is turned with a chain stitch.
Chain 23. Starting in the 2nd chain stitch from the hook.
Rw1: sc across = 22 sts
Rw2: 2»1, 18 sc, 2»1 = 20 sts
Rw3: sc across = 20 sts
Rw4: 2»1, 16 sc, 2»1 = 18 sts
Rw5: sc across = 18 sts

Rw6: 2»1, 14 sc, 2»1 = 16 sts
Rw7: sc across = 16 sts
Rw8: 2»1, 12 sc, 2»1 = 14 sts
Rw9: sc across = 14 sts
Rw10: 2»1, 10 sc, 2»1 = 12 sts
Rw11: sc across = 12 sts
Rw12: 2»1, 8 sc, 2»1 = 10 sts
Rw13: sc across = 10 sts
Rw14: 2»1, 6 sc, 2»1 = 8 sts
Rw15: sc across = 8 sts
Rw16: 2»1, 4 sc, 2»1 = 6 sts
Rw17: sc across = 6 sts

Rw18: 2»1, 2 sc, 2»1 = 4 sts
Rw19: sc across = 4 sts
Rw20: (2»1) x 2 = 2 sts
Rw21: sc across = 2 sts
Rw22: 2»1 = 1 st
Don't break the yarn but continue crocheting around the garland, sc around. In the top two corners, crochet 3 sc in the same stitch. Finish with a slip stitch. Break the yarn and fasten off.

GARLAND

ASSEMBLING

I have placed the pennants in the following order:

· Curry, coral, sea green, light grey, jeans blue and coal
· Light pink, pink, coral, ice blue and petrol blue

With off-white yarn, chain 50. Sc in each stitch at the top of the first pennant. Don't break the yarn, but chain 10, and continue with a sc in each stitch at the top of the next pennant.

Continue like this to the end and finish off by chaining 50.

POPCORN

WHAT YOU WILL NEED

MATERIALS
Off-white cotton
· Drops Safran, color 18

 2.5-3 mm

ABBREVIATIONS
Chain stitch (ch)
Slip stitch (sl st)
Single crochet (sc)
Half double crochet (hdc)
Double crochet (dc)
Increase (2i1)
Decrease (2»1)
Round (R)

POPCORN

· off-white yarn

R1: 6 sc in a magic ring = 6 sts

R2: (2i1) x 6 = 12 sts

R3-4: sc around = 12 sts

R5: (2»1) x 6 = 6 sts

R6: (in the same stitch; 1 hdc, 1 dc, 1 hdc), 1 sl st x 3 = 12 sts

Break the yarn and fasten off.

THANK YOU

It's a strange feeling writing the last page of the book. The last page of my first book, that is. My first book! I have groped in the dark and tried my way. The result has made it all worth it and it's with great pride (and some anxiety) that I'm passing the book along to you. I hope that you will enjoy it.

This book would never have been realized if it wasn't for a lot of people supporting me along the way.

First of all, I would like to thank my amazing family. An eternal support from my sister, Louise Nielsen who has been with me all the way from idea to execution. My mother, Lise Nielsen who always makes sure I stay realistic. My father, Jørgen Madsen who never fails a challenge and helps me to bring all of my projects to life. Thank you all so very much.

Thank you to my amazing team of test crocheters who are behind me. It wouldn't be possible without any of you. You always stand ready to help me. Thank you so much to Susan Seloy, Camilla Vig, Annemarie Pedersen, Tina Gullberg, Kamilla Jensen and Maria Linderod Bülow.

Thank you so much to Christina Bundgaard for editing all of my pictures. You have spent numerous hours on my book and it means the world to me. I have learned so much from you and I hope to learn even more in the future.

Janni Flammild, thank you. Thank you for keeping me sharp and the text in my patterns accurate and for spotting all of my mistakes. I trust you completely and utterly.

A special thanks to Yarnliving.com for supplying all of the yarn used to make this book. And equally as important, thank you for a great cooperation.

Last but not least, thank you to Kandrups Bogtrykkeri, Louise Klit Thomsen and Thomas Thomsen. I have been welcomed with professionalism, positivity and heart warmth. Thank you for meeting all of my expectations and even more. I will definitely use your services for any future projects as well.

SPONSORS AND SUPPLIERS

YARNLIVING.COM
Yarn, crochet hooks

IKEA
Stuffing

PANDURO HOBBY
Feathers, accessories

SOSTRENE GRENE
Accessories

EBAY
Safety eyes

SEWANDSO
Yarn, crochet hooks

INDEX

abbreviations 12
Adorable Ballerina 6, 42–7
arms
   assembly 32, 38, 46, 52, 60, 66,
      74, 80, 88
   crafting 31, 37, 45, 46, 51, 59,
      65, 73, 78, 86
assembly techniques 22, 32, 46, 52,
   60, 66, 74, 80, 88, 94, 100

Ballerina, Adorable 6, 42–7
balls 93
Bear, Little Mr. 6, 28–33
beards 94
bodies
   assembly 32, 38, 46, 52, 60, 66,
      80, 88
   crafting 30, 36, 44, 50, 58, 64, 72,
      78, 86, 92
buns (hair style) 45, 46

clothing 86–7, 88
Clown of the Day 6, 76–81
collars 30, 32
color changes 17
crochet hooks 8
crochet school 14–22

double treble crochet 18–19

ears
   assembly 32, 52, 60, 66, 74
   crafting 31, 51, 59, 64, 73
Elephant Sleepyhead, Mr 6, 56–61
embroidery 32, 36, 38, 46, 60, 66, 80

equipment 8
eyes 60, 93, 94

feather holders 51, 52
fins 92
fish 93
flippers 93, 94

garland 98–101

hair 45, 46, 79, 80, 86, 88
halters 51, 52
hats
   circus 59, 60
   magician's 65, 66
   top 37, 38
heads
   assembly 32, 38, 46, 52, 60, 66,
      80, 88
   crafting 31, 36–7, 44, 50–1, 58–9,
      64, 72, 78, 86
Horse, Shiny Miss 6, 48–51

jackets 36

legs
   crafting 30, 36, 45, 50, 58, 65,
      72, 78, 86
   joining 20–1, 46, 66
Little Miss Magic 6, 62–7
Little Mr Bear 6, 28–33
Little Yellow Lion 6, 19, 70–5

manes 52, 73, 74
materials 8

moustaches 37, 38, 86, 88
Mr Elephant Sleepyhead 6, 56–61
Mr Happy Circus 6, 34–9
Mr Strong 6, 85–9
muzzles 31, 73, 74, 92, 94

noses 46, 73, 74, 79, 80

patterns 10, 26–103
pompoms 16, 60
popcorn 102–3

Shiny Miss Horse 6, 48–51
skirts 44
sleeves 37
stitch markers 10
straps 87
stuffing 22, 32, 38, 46, 52, 60, 66,
   74, 80, 88, 94
suit 86–7, 88
suspenders 79, 80
swimming rings 79, 80

tails 31, 32, 52, 60, 65, 66, 73, 74
trousers 86–7
tusks 92, 94

Walter the Walrus 6, 91–5
weight bars 87
whips 37

yarn 8

A catalogue record for this book is available from the British Library.

ISBN-13: 978-1-4463-0678-9 paperback
SRN: R6958 paperback

ISBN-13: 978-1-4463-7653-9 PDF
SRN: R7114 PDF

ISBN-13: 978-1-4463-7654-6 EPUB
SRN: R7113 EPUB

Printed in China by RR Donnelley for:
F&W Media International, Ltd
Pynes Hill Court, Pynes Hill, Exeter, EX2 5AZ, UK

10 9 8 7 6 5 4 3 2 1

Layout: Kandrups Bogtrykkeri
Photography: Tine Nielsen & Louise Nielsen
Photo editing: Christina Bundgaard Photography
Yarn supplied by Yarnliving.com

F&W Media publishes high quality books on a wide range of subjects.
For more great book ideas visit: **www.sewandso.co.uk**

Layout of the digital edition of this book may vary depending on reader
hardware and display settings.